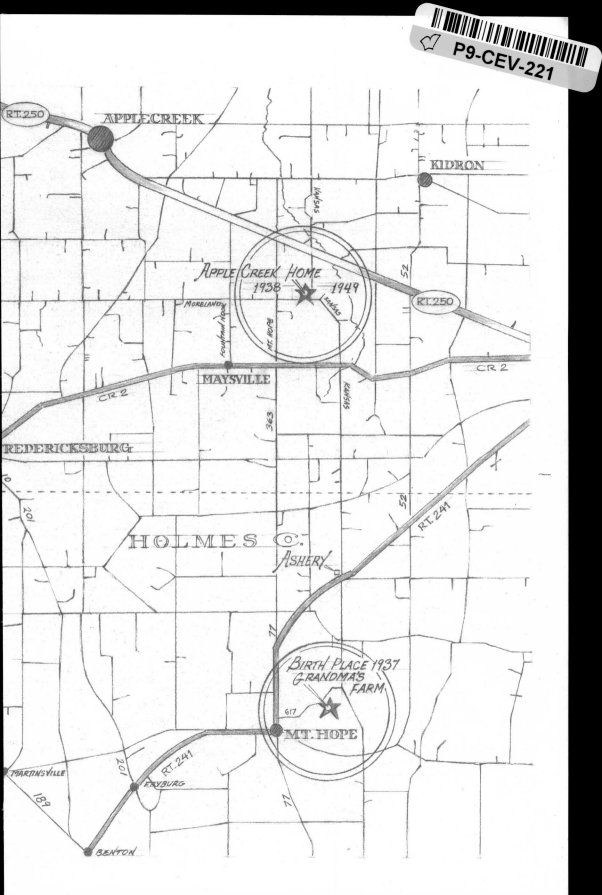

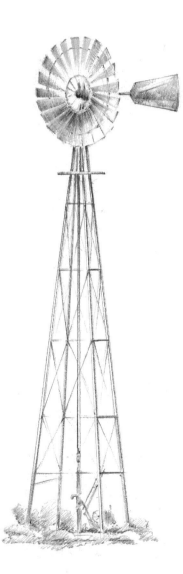

An Amish Boy's Journey

Wayne M. Weaver
with illustrations by Wayne Troyer

The Wooster Book Company
WOOSTER • OHIO

921
WEAVER

The Wooster Book Company, Wooster Ohio 44691

Published in the United States of America.
Second Printing

ISBN 1-888683-37-6

Library of Congress Cataloging-In-Publication Data
Weaver, Wayne M. , 1937–
    Dust between my toes : an Amish boy's journey / Wayne M. Weaver,
        with illustrations by Wayne Troyer.
                    p.   cm.
    ISBN 1-888683-37-6 (case : alk. paper)
    1. Weaver, Wayne M., 1937–   .
    2. Physicians—United States—Biography.
    3. Amish—Social life and customs.
I. Title.
R154.W2993A3   1996
610' .92—dc21
[B]
                                                96-39479
                                                CIP

♾ This book is printed on acid-free paper.
Book designed by The Wooster Book Company
& printed at

CARLISLE
PRESS
WALNUT CREEK
2727 Press Run Road · Sugarcreek, OH 44681

Thanks

The people who helped bring this writing to fruition in a special way are my wife, LaVina Miller Weaver, and my mother, Elizabeth Schlabach Weaver. I also relied on my brothers Roy, Dan, and Monroe Jr. ("Buckwheat") to verify some of my early childhood recollections. All four of our children; David, Mark, Mary, and Lois contributed to the book. A special thanks goes to David Wiesenberg for shepherding the entire writing, editing, and publishing process. The book would not have been possible without the counsel and editing help provided by David and Elsie Kline and by Fran Mast. I also wish to thank Dennis Kline and his sister Marie Kline for the final proofreading, and Marvin Wengerd and the Carlisle Printing staff for printing the book. Mona Hershberger (Pifer Jake's Mona) was very helpful in providing neighborhood information and confirming dates in the early part of the book. Many of the people who have worked on this project are from the Amish community. Their erudition, resourcefulness, and attention to detail are to be much admired.

I am truly indebted for the warmth, feeling, and insight that the pencil sketches contribute to the story. After the artist, Wayne Troyer, read the manuscript we each made a list of places in the story we felt could benefit from a sketch. The items we had in common are the sketches in the book. In every instance, the finished sketches exceed my expectations. The artist's childhood had much in common with mine. In addition to growing up in an Amish home, Wayne's mother Clara is my first cousin. Clara's mother, the artist's grandmother, was my father's oldest sister Ada. You will meet Ada later, as a young teenager visiting the St. Louis Zoo.

Dust Between My Toes: An Amish Boy's Journey

List of Illustrations:

Wayne Troyer

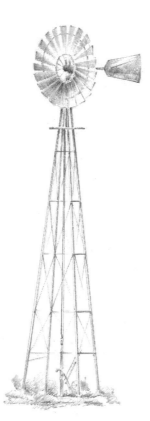

Opening Remarks

PSYCHOLOGISTS TELL US THAT WHO WE ARE IS DETERMINED by a combination of factors. They say our gene pool, the teachings of our parents, our upbringing and our environment determine who we are. The environment, they go on to explain, includes our education, what we see and read, and the people with whom we associate. I acknowledge that all of these are important in fashioning us into who we are. However, I believe that our destiny in this life and in the next are determined by our spiritual essence. I believe this, even though my life has all too often failed to embrace the spiritual within me. Having said this, I wish to mention several people, other than my family, whose lives and works have, in a special way, motivated and inspired me.

H. Lester Houff was a model and mentor to me in the formative years of my professional life. Mr. Houff, known to his friends as H.L., was a Virginia farmer and businessman from northern Augusta County. He grew up and lived in the Weyers Cave area. For many years, in addition to farming, he owned and operated a thrashing rig and a chicken-egg-and-cream route. In the Depression years, his trucking enterprise grew from a cream-and-egg route to include livestock brokering and, eventually, the transport of other commercial goods. With the help of his family, especially his son Cletus, the family business grew over the next several decades into a large trucking firm. Since the death of H.L. and Cletus, the business is being operated by Cletus' sons Dwight and Doug. The home office is located in Weyers Cave, with terminals in many of the larger cities in the middle Atlantic states. My wife and I value our continued relationship with the Houff family.

Mutual friendship probably best describes the relationship with Rudy and Doris Soldan. Other than my immediate family, the Soldans have been my best friends over recent years. They and their son Rick lived just outside Mount Crawford, Virginia, when I first met them in 1975. Rudy had just retired from the United States State Department as a Foreign Service officer. While stationed in Moscow, Rudy was attacked and badly beaten by Russian guards at the United States Embassy. Subsequent to the beating, he had a heart attack. Following his recovery from the heart attack, Rudy was assigned to Manilla in the Philippines. After he returned to the States from Manilla, Rudy retired on a medical disability. After returning to the States, they retired to their Mount Crawford, Virginia home.

Rudy came to the United States from Czechoslovakia at the age of fifteen. His mother, a widow, had immigrated earlier. Rudy's life in the United States started as a baker in New York City. After recovering from injuries he suffered in World War II in the Battle of the Bulge, Rudy was recruited by the United States State Department. He completed the required training and began his life's career first as a Foreign Service Staff Officer and was later commissiond by the Congress. Rudy speaks seven languages. The Soldans were stationed in various United States embassies all over the world during his career. Some of the stories of their experiences from those years are, to say the least, spellbinding.

My respect and admiration for the generation of doctors prior to my generation has only increased over the years. I have had the opportunity to sit and listen to people like Dr. Luther High and Dr. Owen Patterson talk about the way things were in the '30s, '40s, and '50s. Dr. High told me what it was like to get stuck in the snow, twelve times one winter, between Mount Hope and Bunker Hill, Ohio. Those were the days of one dollar office visits and two dollar house calls. Baby cases, as they were called, cost twenty dollars. Dr. High tells of losing several baby cases one year to a newcomer to the practice of medicine in the county. After the new doctor found out what the going rate for baby cases was, he underbid the other doctors by charging only eighteen dollars. The house calls he made, starting out in an automobile, but often completed in a buggy or sleigh, are too numerous to mention.

My favorite authors are James A. Michener, Allan W. Eckert and Mark Twain. Their writings have, I am sure, over the years influenced my interests in history, geography, and people. Although I have read nearly all of Tom Clancy's books, I sometimes come away with just a tinge of guilt. His writings try my rule to limit my reading to material that is useful and informative in real life. Some of his writings also test a second rule: to not read material that I would be uncomfortable recommending to my friends and family. My favorite newspaper columnist is George F. Will.

At least one biography of many of the prominent public figures over the last forty years is in my library. A habit I acquired as a young grade-schooler—reading two newspapers a day—has remained with me throughout my adult life. I still consider this the cornerstone of my education.

Numbered among the acquaintances I have who grew up in Amish settings similar to mine are at least six other medical doctors and many nurses. The group also includes two commercial airline pilots and many businessmen and women, as well as other professional people. One of the pilots, Gideon Miller, was recently killed in the TWA flight 800 crash catastrophe. He was a member of the church my wife and I attend when we are in Sarasota, Florida. Another pilot, Myron Stoltzfus, flies for American Airlines. His routes take him to Europe and South America mostly. His family attended Weavertown, the Beachy Amish church we attended during my residency years at Lancaster General Hospital in Lancaster, Pennsylvania.

I cherish the many Amish friends I have, who are more learned than I am in various fields, and yet, have no formal education beyond the eighth grade. Education, I believe, is as much about attitude as about formal, didactic material.

Preface

MY PARENTS, MONROE AND ELIZABETH WEAVER, BELONGED to the Old Order Amish faith. At the time of my birth in the summer of 1937 they were living on Grandmother's farm near Mount Hope, Ohio. I was the third child; two brothers, Roy, two, and Dan, one, preceded me. Uncle Isaac has frequently reminded me that he made bicycle trips to Mount Hope two nights in a row the week I was born. The first one, early one evening, was for Frank Shoup the veterinarian. My parents' favorite driving mare, Queen, had problems foaling. The second night's trip was to call Dr. Mitchell to attend my birth.

When I was six months old, my family moved from Grandmother's farm in Holmes County to a small seventeen acre farm in Salt Creek Township, Wayne County. This was my home for the next eleven years and the setting for the first part of this book. The rest of my growing up years took place on the farm we moved to, west of Holmesville, Ohio, in 1949. My father

Grandma's home where I was born,
near Mount Hope in Holmes County Ohio

passed away in May, 1993. My mother, at age eighty-three, lives in the *daudy* house on the home place with a granddaughter. One of her grandsons and his family live in the farmhouse.

I am now a *Daudy* (grandfather) to eight grandchildren. The oldest ones are beginning to show an interest in their heritage. The "*Daudy, when you were a little boy*" questions, along with prompting from my children, my wife LaVina, and friends got this manuscript started. These stories of childhood recollections and life experiences are the result. When the initial plans for a forty to fifty page booklet got out of hand, a book ensued. Like most people I know, my life has had its good and bad times. It is hoped the readers of these memoirs see me, for the most part, as a participant on a journey that took some unexpected turns.

Amish children are taught that the pursuit of individual acclaim, including talking and writing about one's self, is unbecoming to those claiming the faith. It appears that I have internalized this tenet sufficiently to have experienced some uneasiness and hesitation before getting started on my memoirs. In many respects, it was reassuring to realize that thirty-five years haven't distanced me from the values taught to me as a child. I shared these misgivings with David Kline, an Amish farmer and writer. He assured me that he was well acquainted with the feeling. He told me that one's attitude and purpose can always be second-guessed.

I hope these memoirs pass the attitude-and-purpose litmus test for its readers.

Pifer Jakes' place

Childhood and Elementary Years

IT WAS 1943, THE SPRING BEFORE MY SIXTH BIRTHDAY. I FELT quite important waiting for Pifer Katie to come to the door. This was the first time I was sent on an errand to the neighbors. It was planting season and we needed to ask our neighbor, Jacob Hershberger, known as Pifer Jake, if we could borrow a team to till a field for strawberries. We wanted to arrange for the horses before they were turned out to pasture for the day. It was early in the spring and as my feet got cold, I reminded myself that I was already five, and anyone big enough to run an errand like this shouldn't mind cold feet. My two brothers, seven and eight, had to go to school that morning. They walked to school with the other neighbor children as they came by our house.

On this April day, our family included Father, thirty-four years old, Mother, thirty, Roy, eight, Dan, seven, the writer, five, Ada, four, Fannie, three, and Monroe Jr., two. Amanda, an infant, had died two months earlier, at nine months of age.

Mother's sisters, Mary Ann and Amanda, helped so much with the housework and caring for the children, they were considered family too. We all wore traditional Amish clothes made by my mother on a foot treadle sewing machine. About the only clothes we bought were underwear, socks, and headgear. My father's presence gave our home a sense of security. As I remember it, my home was an orderly, disciplined place. That was so without a great deal of effort. I don't recall Father ever being angry or unkind with my mother. My father didn't like slothfulness or the appearance of it. He admonished us to always walk like we were going somewhere, and do our work as if it was worth doing.

I was usually allowed to sleep-in in the morning, at least until my two brothers went to school. This morning was different; there was an errand to do. As my feet got colder, I knocked on Pifer Jake's door again. Just then, I heard Katie coming from the barn where she had been milking. She had a way with children. She assured me that I was pretty big to run such an early morning errand. On this morning she gave me a cookie. The cookie was good, but I was hoping for one of her good half-moon *schnitz* pies. When she turned to the cupboard instead of the blue pantry door, I knew it would be a cookie that morning. She read my note and after assuring herself that I was warm, she saw me out the lane. A few minutes later, I arrived home with a note for Father clutched in my hand. That summer I was assigned other chores. The first one was to keep a cardboard box behind the kitchen stove filled with corncobs.

Values were primarily taught by example. I do recall that the distinction between "acting honest" and "being honest" was taught by using the biblical example of Ananias and Sapphira in the Book of Acts. As a young child, I was taught a lesson about promises and promise-keeping because of neglecting to do a chore I had agreed to do for my grandmother. Ten cents' worth of kindness and help, I was told, is worth far more than the grandest promises or good intentions.

We lived at a country crossroads, which meant other roads brought children past our house on their way to school. This made for a lot of exciting news when the boys came home from school each day. We found out who had a new calf or colt, new puppies or kittens, or a new brother or sister. The boys were the information exchange for the eight to ten families going by our house to school.

My father operated a feed mill and ran the small dairy and poultry farm we lived on. Pifer Jakes lived a quarter of a mile away, down a lane, off the road going east. Mona Daves lived on the next farm along the east road. Katie, Pifer Jake's wife, was a sister to my grandmother. Mona Dave's wife, Tina, was also Grandmother's sister. Johnson School was about a half mile up the west road at the next crossroads. Jewel Bupp lived in a lane to the north before you got to Johnson School. Just past Bupp's lane along the south side of the road was the Urie Gingerich farm. Mona Gingerich lived on the first farm on the road going north. Just beyond their farm, at the crossroads for US Route 250, was the blacksmith shop. Abe Shetler, the blacksmith, and his family lived next door.

Pifer Mona recently reminded me of the way they, and some of the local farmers, got their horses home from the blacksmith after shoeing. The farmer or his son would leave the horses at the blacksmith shop in the morning. After the horses were shod, Abe started them on the road back to the farm and released them. Some time later, depending on the distance, the horses appeared at their owner's barn door.

Danny D.'s John lived on the first farm to the south. The south road was actually a lane that went on to connect with

Childhood home near Apple Creek in Wayne County Ohio

what is now Harrison Road near Maysville.

Bupp's bush (woods) was to the north of the feed mill just beyond the pasture field. A rail fence separated the woods from the road. A small half-rotted stump just across the fence from our pasture field provided a favorite place to watch red squirrels and chipmunks. The rail fence served as a race track for them. The small creek running from Bupp's bush through a culvert and into Pifer Jake's bush on the other side of the road provided our first fishing hole. A curved straight pin was tied on the end of a piece of string and a small willow branch served as the pole. Catching minnows with worms as bait was a delightful way to while away warm summer days. On an earlier visit to Grandmother's house at Mount Hope, Aunt Mary Ann had shown us how to make the fishing lines. She also took us to the creek below Grandmother's house to show us how to make use of an old window screen to catch minnows.

I always felt a little miffed about the birth of my younger brothers and sisters. Somehow the birth of my younger brother, Eli, was the only one for which I was prepared. Eli was also the only one born in a hospital. The births of Mary Ann, Lester, Amanda, and Monroe Jr. were total surprises to me. Father always brought us the news. Either Mona Dave Tina or Pifer Katie were usually present and served as midwife assistant to the doctor. On each occasion, I clearly remember the hushed, escorted trip to the bedroom where we found Mother propped up in bed and holding a tiny new infant. If the births took place during the day, we were either in school or taken over to Pifer Jake's. If the births were at night, we awoke to the unexpected surprise in the morning.

A schoolmate from Fountain Nook days recently told me of his experience. One late spring day when he was ten, his father sent him to their large hay field to turn already dry, wind rowed hay with a pitchfork. He was greatly puzzled. A side rake and team could do in an hour or two what he estimated would take him at least a week if done by hand as fast as he could. The puzzle was solved several hours later when he was called to the house to meet his new baby brother.

As I recall, church services and religious life seemed as much a part of our community, as a personal part of our family. We had daily morning and evening prayer, with the family kneeling and Father praying out loud. The evening prayer was read in German from a devotional prayer book. The morning prayer was, for the most part, spontaneous. There was always silent prayer before and after meals. Our church services, including the singing, were all in high German and lasted three or four hours. Worship services were held every other Sunday at one of the homes in the congregation. During the warm weather season, they were held in the barn. The upstairs wagon or thrasher-den floor served as the sanctuary. It was cleaned with special care for the occasion. Neighbors and relatives often helped clean and get ready for church. During the summer months we went to church in our bare feet.

Mows of hay often formed the side borders of the area used for services in the barn. Rows of benches ran the length of the den floor, with the women on one side facing the men on the other side. The space between the men and the women formed an aisle three to five feet wide. The ministers stood at the far end of this aisle away from the barn door opening. These doors were open or closed depending on the weather. On what we referred to as "no-church Sunday," we had stories from the Bible or *Martyr's Mirror* read to us in the forenoon. At other times, we attended services in neighboring congregations, or spent the day visiting with family and friends. This often meant a short buggy ride and good food for the day. Except for the chores involving the animals, there was no Sunday work.

Having church services in the home was a custom started by necessity in the early Anabaptist movement. When the Swiss Brethren, the precursors of the Amish, withdrew from the state church in the early sixteenth century, they were severely persecuted. They initially met in their homes. When this was outlawed, they started meeting in barns, woods, and sometimes in caves. The persecutors were the leaders of the state churches. This led to mistrusting much of what the state religions represented, including a distrust of the hierarchical nature of the state church, as well as a dislike for their large cathedrals. The Amish church of today still reflects these aversions.

My first recollection of a church service was in Pifer Jake's barn. I'm not sure, but I would guess I was three years old. We three oldest boys sat with Father. In those days, the seating consisted of benches with peg legs and no back. Today the bench legs have spring loaded hinges to let them fold flat under the seat. At this age, the younger children got a mid-service cookie and milk intermission. Usually, my oldest brother Roy escorted me to the house for this break.

On this Sunday, I was sitting on Father's lap and fell asleep. Later I awoke, lying on the bench, with my head in his lap. The sermon was going on in German. The preacher's voice was coming from the direction of the granary. When I couldn't identify its source, my young mind concluded it was *da Gute Mon* talking from the granary. Amish children call God "*da Gute Mon.*" This is best translated as *benevolent creator* and *Lord*. I don't recall being greatly puzzled. It seems I was more bewildered later when I learned the voice wasn't God's. A simple noon meal was always served after the church services. Sometimes there was bean soup, made with bread and milk. This was one of my favorite dishes, but that of course doesn't include the desserts, where *schnitz* pie reigned supreme.

Following Father from the feed mill to the chicken house, then to the barn, was a part of a preschool day, unless there was bad weather. Watering and feeding the livestock and chickens didn't seem monotonous to me. I remember playing around Father's desk when he did bookkeeping work. In the early years, a day always included make-believe work, play, and imposed naps. In the house, besides play, watching sewing, baking, washing and ironing, and other household tasks was the main pastime. Riding Bert, a draft horse, while cultivating the produce patch with a one-horse cultivator, is probably the first direct contact I had with a horse. I was three or four years old and just along for the ride. Bert was a large Belgian draft mare that belonged to Pifer Jakes.

One of our early tasks was going to the Bupp's to make telephone calls for Father. We had a pony to ride, or could drive in a cart for errands like this. We took a written note for Doris, Jewel's wife, or Mildred, Lavern's wife, and they would place the call for us on a wall mounted crank telephone while we waited. We often went with Father to deliver hay, feed, and grains to local farmers. I recall going with Father to the harness shop, blacksmith shop, and buggy shop as a preschooler. These shops were all within several miles of our home.

During the decade of the '40s we raised from one-and-a-half to two acres of strawberries each year. About the time we started school we were given the opportunity to earn money picking berries. After showing we could pick clean and stay at it, we were allowed in the strawberry patch with the other pickers, for pay. We got one penny per quart for picking. Father considered Pifer Katie and her daughter Edna as models for strawberry pickers. Of the children, my sister Ada was the best picker. I recall one day when she picked over fifty quarts as an eight or nine year old. That day, Father explained to us that the money Ada earned was the same amount he got paid on some days during the Depression. Father talked of one Amish farmer, Eli Kurtz, whom he worked for during the Depression. They worked hard all day hauling manure. When the man paid Father, he told him that he was ashamed to pay him only a dollar, and gave him a dollar and a half.

On days the strawberries couldn't all be sold near home, we had to peddle them in Wooster or Massillon. I first helped with this the summer I was six. Father bought money changers that we hung on our pants' top. We practiced using them during the evenings after work. Most of the time, Jewel Bupp or his son Lavern—neighbors to the west—provided our transportation to Wooster. The strawberries were hauled in the trunk of Bupp's car or truck. Bupp would drive the car, with open trunk, along the street and park after an intersection. We would walk down to the first five or six houses of the intersecting streets, as well as both sides of the street the car was on. Father would get the berries out of the crates and fix trays of six quarts. We carried them house to house, ringing doorbells or knocking on doors. We got quite good at making change for up to a five dollar bill. The berries sold for twenty to thirty cents a quart. Years later when Lovina and I moved into our house on Nold Avenue, I recognized the place as one where I had peddled berries fifteen years earlier.

When I was five, Father taught the three oldest of us how to trap muskrats. We got permission to trap along Little Salt Creek where it crossed Pifer Jake's farm. The creek ran across the whole width of their farm. Trapping meant getting up at four in the morning. Cold, dark, and often wet or snowy mornings were the rule. The traps were set the night the season opened in late fall. After the first week or so, the trap-line became our project.

We carried a kerosene lantern and flashlight for light. The traps needed to be set with minimal ground disturbance and positioned so that the muskrats would drown when they were caught. We caught over thirty muskrats the first year. After catching them, they had to be skinned, stretched, and dried before being sold. The first winter's catch was sold to Benny Amstutz in Kidron. Our pelts earned us nearly a hundred dollars. These proceeds were divided among the three of us. With this and the strawberry-picking money, a savings account was started for each of us at the Mount Eaton Bank.

The summer I was first allowed in the strawberry patch was the same year I started to school. We went to a one-room school that had one teacher for all eight grades. In our home, and church community, everyone spoke Pennsylvania Dutch, a German dialect, so preparation for school called for informal English lessons at home. Father had a lot of public contact with non-Amish people in his feed business. We called non-Amish people "*hocha lade*," high people. This contact and our strawberry selling experiences helped the language preparation efforts for school. All but two families in our school were Amish and those children could talk Pennsylvania Dutch. Each year, first graders arrived at school unable to speak English. The schoolbooks were in English and the teacher couldn't talk Pennsylvania Dutch. With the exception of a personal experience of my own, I don't recall anyone not making the transition to English. That incident will be touched on later.

The first paddling I recall receiving occurred when I was four. Our farm neighbor, Urie Gingerich, was tiling a field across the road from our house. Their boys were following the ditching machine with a team and wagon, laying clay tiles along the side of the trench. Father gave my oldest brother Roy permission to go with them on the wagon. I was told to stay on our side of the road. When Father left, I went for what I thought would be a clandestine trip across the road. But it didn't turn out that way. It took me only a short time to break a tile. The outcome was a paddling which took place on the back porch that evening. Even though my mother assures me that I got my share of paddlings, that is the only one I remember. Two years later, my grandparents, Atlee and Fannie Wengerd Weaver, bought three acres of land off the field across the road and built a small *daudy* house. Grandfather worked for my father for the next seven years. Grandmother was sick and bedridden this entire time. We spent a lot of time at their house. I have never forgotten that their house is built over the spot where I had broken the tile.

Other childhood recollections include sitting on bags of feed, in the mill, with the noise of grinding and mixing going on. My brothers and I liked to sit on these stacks of white cotton bags. The bags contained feed concentrates for mixing dairy, hog, or chicken feeds. The farmers brought their grain, often ear corn, or sometimes shelled corn, wheat, or other grains to the mill. They backed their wagons or hacks under the mill overhang to unload their grain. After Father processed their orders, grinding the grain and adding the concentrates and minerals they wanted, the feed was mixed and bagged, and loaded back on the wagons. One of our jobs was holding the feed bags while Father filled them with feed or grain. He used a scoop shovel to fill the bags. But back to the feed bags themselves; Mother used these white cotton bags for making us boys "everyday" shirts. She prepared the cotton material by washing and bleaching the bags a number of times. This softened the material and disguised the lettering on the bags. She used the same material to make slips for the girls.

Another vivid memory occurred in the mill several years

later. One of the hired hands that helped in the mill smoked. One day, for some reason, he started to leave his cigarettes on top of the desk in the mill office. It wasn't too long before two of us found ourselves unable to resist the temptation. Dan and I went behind the chicken house and lit and shared a smoke. We also shared the nausea that followed. I never asked my father, but I always wondered if this was a setup he had something to do with.

Another tobacco related incident involved Berry Jonas' Andy coming to shear our sheep. He arrived one morning in his horse drawn hack with a gas powered engine and shearing attachments in the back. Soon after, we were standing in awe watching the sheep losing their woolen fleeces to the smooth strokes of Andy's shears. After the shearing novelty wore off, a friendly banter between Andy and us got underway. We were soon on the topic of chewing tobacco. My attempt to exhibit my worldly wisdom on the finer points of chewing tobacco soon turned into a put-up or shut-up offer. Either take a chew or admit I really don't know what I was talking about. The outcome was—the day for this eight year old ended in misery in bed.

In the preschool years, I went with Father to unload grain from railroad cars at Apple Creek. Part of the feed business also included selling lime and fertilizer. Going along on deliveries got me acquainted with nearly all the roads within four or five miles of our home. These excursions left me with a sense of distance and direction. My sense of the earth being large and round was completed on a visit to Lake Erie. Here Father pointed out the reason ships seemed to disappear over the horizon.

Friendly competition was a part of just about everything we did in both work and play. One of our favorite rivalries was knowing where all the farm and household products we used were made. As a young grade-schooler, I learned that Nabisco's Shredded Wheat was made in Niagara Falls, New York and that Kellogg's Corn Flakes came from Battle Creek, Michigan.

I remember the first butchering I attended. On a late fall or early winter morning, we went to Pifer Jake's where they already had kettles full of boiling water over wood fires. My parents wouldn't let me watch the actual hog killing. One of the adults dispatched them with a bullet to the head. I do recall a year or two later, the feeling in the pit of my stomach when I first saw what a well placed bullet did to a full grown steer or cow. The instantaneous buckling of all four legs of this large animal, following a not very loud snap of a .22 caliber rifle, left me with a serious respect for guns and bullets.

After the hogs were killed and bled, they were dipped into a large wooden trough filled with boiling water from the kettles. From the trough, the carcass was rolled with ropes onto a wooden platform where the hair was scraped off. From the platform, they were hung from tripod poles. After disemboweling, the carcass was cut and sawed in half by splitting the backbone. The halves were then put on large tables to be cut into hams, shoulders, and slabs of bacon. While this work was being done, mostly by the men, the women took the small intestines and, after a cleaning process, stripped the transparent inner lining out. This was used as casing for sausage. Our home had its own "environmental protection agency." It was simple—use everything until it's worn out. Don't waste anything.

Shoulders and other meat parts not used for hams and bacon were ground into sausage. The sausage was stuffed into the casing directly from the grinder. The first sausage grinder I recall was powered by a small gasoline engine. My parents told us that their earlier ones were hand cranked. The carcass fat was saved to boil down in a rendering process, making lard. The

hams and bacon went to the smokehouse. Meat from boiling the head and feet and other leftover scraps was ground and mixed with cornmeal to make panhaas. Bits of crisp fat left over from the rendering process were called cracklings. Bits of bowel, when fried hard in the rendering process, resulted in chitlins. Both of these were eaten with a little salt. Writing this recollection of past butchering days reminds me what people miss when they buy all their meat at the grocery store.

My parents had zero tolerance for any offending behavior towards people who "were different." Since we rarely interacted with people of other races this was usually in reference to people with physical or mental handicaps. Farm living in those days taught one a distinct appreciation and understanding of the realities of life. Life wasn't always fair, but it was real. A kicking horse had to be dealt with differently than a compliant one. If you insisted on treating them the same you suffered the consequences. In dealing with our farm animals, we were made keenly aware of the distinction between cruelty and necessary compliance. Good people, we were taught, didn't beat or hurt animals and always fed them well.

Most of our neighbors had windmills to pump their water. There were some hand dug wells, but for the most part, the wells were drilled. Some farms had springs strong enough to supply water for the home and livestock. A minority used small engines for pumping water. On the farm we moved to when I was eleven, we had an artesian well about two hundred and fifty yards downhill from the house. Father capped the well to harness the flow and power a water wheel. A heavy wire ran from the water wheel to a drilled well in our yard. The water wheel ran day and night, summer and winter. It pumped water to a trough in our summer kitchen. Most of the Amish homes I knew had a summer house or basement that was cooler and where the cooking and canning were done through the warm months. This continuous flow of fresh water was used for refrigeration to keep the food cool. Additionally, in the summer, we had an icebox for things that needed to be kept colder. Ice was delivered to the house twice a week. There were four ice block sizes to choose from, twenty-five, fifty, seventy-five, and one hundred pounds. A stiff square piece of cardboard, with the different block sizes, was set in a front window to tell the iceman how much ice was needed. This saved him an extra trip to the house at each stop. We usually got a one hundred pound block. The iceman lifted the block to his shoulder with an ice tong. Most of the icemen had a stiff leather sheath to protect their shoulder from direct contact with the ice. If less than one hundred pounds was needed, he used an ice pick to split the block into halves or quarters.

But back to the water supply; the water flowed from the house to the chicken house by gravity, and from there to the milk house, barn, and hog house in that order. We had a separate water supply for the hot water heater and for washing and cleaning purposes in the house and barn. This supply came from rain water diverted from the roof to a holding cistern. A small gasoline engine was used to pump and keep this water under pressure in a tank in the basement. We had a natural gas well on the farm that was used for heating water and for brooding newly hatched chicks and newborn pigs.

Each summer, thrashing was an anticipated community event. From six to ten farmers in a neighborhood formed what was called a thrashing ring. When one farmer's job was completed, the thrashing machine and crew moved on to the next farm. In my earliest memories of thrashing, power was provided by steam. We would first hear the steam engine whistle followed by smoke on the horizon. This would let the farmers in our thrashing ring know to get their team and wagons ready. Later, the thrashing machines were powered by gasoline or diesel tractors. A forty to fifty-foot drive belt transferred the power from the engine to the thrashing machine.

Our thrasher ring usually had four wagons to haul the shocked wheat to the barn. Sometime before lunch, the meals became a topic of discussion by the field hands. Wheat and oats were the major small grains thrashed. Barley and rye made up a smaller portion. Some of the same farms that thrashed small grains also filled silos. For these farms there was a silo fillers' ring. Since we had a silo, we participated in both rings. Handling bundles of green corn for silo filling was heavy work. Carrying cold drinks to the loaders in the field and bringing the message to come for lunch were early chores we children performed on thrashing and silo filling days. We were exposed to the work of these crews for a number of years before becoming active participants. Going thrashing the first time was an eagerly anticipated event.

One summer, as a second or third grader during thrashing season, I got the job of pushing oats away from the thrashing machine spout. The work took place in the granary while thrashing at Pifer Jake's. I wore a large red bandanna tied around my face to avoid the dust. On this occasion, there was a bumper oats crop that produced over a hundred bushels an acre. As the granary bin filled up, it got harder and harder to keep the oats pushed away. Each hopper dumped one-half bushel. By the time the tractor power was turned down, signaling an empty wagon, I was frantic with fear. I thought sure I would suffocate under the rising pile of oats. Before the next load, Daniel Yoder, the thrasher foreman, came to the granary. He kindly explained to me that I should have come to him when the oats started piling up. My not getting hurt was more impor-

tant than the thrashing machine getting plugged up. This was the same granary I had thought God was talking from several years earlier.

In my earliest years, we had a cast-iron bell on top of the house. A rope ran from the bell down through the upstairs walls and ended behind one of the bedroom doors downstairs. This was only used for bad weather days or other special occasions. The bell had an interesting and, to us, scary history.

In 1932, six years before we moved to this house, a widower, Joni Byler, and his daughter lived there. One night, strangers came to the house and bound the two, hand and foot, and demanded all their money. They poured kerosene on the floor around them. When the strangers were told where the money was they weren't satisfied with the amount and threatened to set the home on fire. After Joni and his daughter repeatedly explained that that was all they had at the house, and pleaded for their lives, the robbers left. By backing up to each other on the floor, they eventually freed themselves and went to Pifer Jake's. They slept at Pifer Jake's for a number of weeks after that.

Mr. Byler then hired a carpenter to make and install a bell tower with a bell on top of the house. This was to be rung in case of an emergency. After the Bylers moved away, Mona Dave's Sam and his wife lived there. One night, Pifer Jake awoke to the bell's ring. He awakened his two oldest sons and all three went to see what the problem was. They were expecting the worst and were relieved to find the problem to be Sam, sick in bed. Several of them went to the Bupp farm to call for the doctor. After a house call, the doctor had him taken to the hospital in Wooster, where he was operated on for a ruptured appendix.

Recently, the Chupp family—now living in my old child-hood home— were nice enough to invite my wife and me on a tour of the house. Behind the bedroom door was the plaster-patched hole through which the end of Joni Byler's bell rope dangled fifty-five years earlier. Just off the kitchen as we came in from the back porch still stood our uniquely constructed wash sink. It is only 18 to 20 inches off the floor, but it is larger and deeper than an ordinary wash basin. Father had it custom-made so we children could comfortably stand at the basin to wash our faces and hands when coming in from work or play. It was also constructed so that we could sit on the rim with our feet in the sink for nightly feet scrubbing duty during the warm weather months. I suspect that if the opportunity were given, two generations of Chupp children would have a similar story of washing up to tell.

The sink brought to mind a sort of constant low-grade dispute between Mother and Aunt Mary Ann about how our feet went to bed. We children not only had our nightly foot check before bedtime but had to pass the washing-versus-rinsing inquiry. I could never figure out how the adults could make a judgment about whether we had washed or only rinsed while sitting forty feet away in the living room reading the newspaper. It took me awhile, but I eventually resolved to wash my feet correctly the first time.

The sink was also the checkpoint on school days and on Sunday mornings for scrutinizing behind our ears and around our collars for dirt. Somehow the adults were not impressed by our argument that what they claimed was dirt was just a good suntan.

During the winter, we had a large wood and coal stove in the living room that stayed fired up day and night. This stove had a hole in the ceiling above it that was boxed in with registers to let heat get upstairs to the children's sleeping rooms. The kitchen stove fire usually went out during the night. This had to be restarted each morning, not only to cook and bake, but to heat

the kitchen end of the house during the day. It also had a water reservoir at one end to heat water for household use. Dried corncobs and kerosene were used to start the fire. Once the fire was started, wood kindling was added. For serious firing, which was needed in baking and canning, coal was used.

I recall an early lesson about responsibility from the winter I was a first grader. Because I played too long, it got dark one evening before I got the corncob box filled. At five o'clock the next morning, Mother wanted to kindle a fire and there were no corncobs. We slept upstairs where it got quite cold during the winter. I was roused out of bed onto the cold floor for a memorable trip through the dark to the mill for corncobs. A flashlight served for light. This only happened once and left me with a sense of what happens when people shirk their responsibility. Several years later I was deemed big and responsible enough to keep the coal buckets filled for both stoves.

Chores were the proving grounds for learning about work and work habits. Here is where I learned it was easier to carry two buckets of water three-quarters full than one filled to the brim. We learned the most efficient and quickest way to get a job done. Innovation wasn't penalized or hampered by regulations. As we boys were being taught to do the outside chores, Mother, Aunt Mary Ann, or one of the other aunts were teaching my sisters housekeeping, cooking, and needle work. The latter included sewing, patching clothes, crocheting, and embroidering.

Not having a car, electricity, or a telephone was part of Amish life. I don't recall giving this much thought until I was a teenager. My two older brothers and I had our first train ride when I was three or four years old. Father took the three of us to Apple Creek, Ohio where we caught a train to Orrville, Ohio. I recall Father transacting some business in Orrville while we boys waited for the return train to Apple Creek. Recently, Pifer

Jake's Mona, who lives about two miles from my present home, confirmed this train trip. He recalled Father telling him a short time before we took the trip, "The boys are begging for a train ride. One of these days when it suits," he told Mona, "I will take them to the Apple Creek station for a ride to either Millersburg or Orrville."

In the winter of 1943, before my fifth birthday, I went with my father on a train trip to Maryland and Virginia. We visited Amish and Mennonite young men who were in Civilian Public Service. As conscientious objectors to military service they served in this program instead of serving in the military. When the young Amish boys in our community reached the age of eighteen, they had to register with their local draft boards. My father helped them fill out these applications. It was the process by which they got their conscientious objector classification from the draft board.

In the darkness of a cold winter night, Jewel Bupp took us to catch the train from the station in Apple Creek. I remember standing at the railroad station under Father's cape overcoat. From there I watched the huge noisy steam engine come hissing and puffing into the station. The train was nearly full of soldiers, with many passengers having to stand. I recall being afraid of the soldiers. When Father got too tired to hold me, I had to stand and hold onto his leg. A soldier offered to hold me but I was too scared at first to accept his offer. When I became tired, with Father's approval and encouragement, I accepted the offer and sat on the soldier's lap. I remember being surprised to find him a kind and gentle man. Father had to stand all the way to Pittsburgh and was also grateful for the offer. I clearly remember the noise, smell, and jolting of the train cars through the night. On the train, and at the train station in Pittsburgh, I first saw black people. I recall the conductor's announcements, "All

Train Station in Apple Creek Ohio

aboard for Pittsburgh!"

To my recollection, I always have had a fascination for trains. I recall when the first diesel engines coming through Apple Creek were a topic receiving attention. The train track from Apple Creek ran past Father's uncle Harry's farm—which was located between Apple Creek and Fredericksburg. A year or two earlier, on a Sunday afternoon visit to their place, Harry's boys put pennies on the rails and gave us each a flat metal railroad souvenir.

On this trip, we changed trains in Pittsburgh during the night. I recall Hagerstown, Maryland; Front Royal, Virginia; and Luray and Grottoes, Virginia, as places we stopped. At Hagerstown we met a friend of Father's who was a feed salesman. He took us to Boonsboro and several other towns in the area. I remember large apple orchards along the road. This was the first time I saw mountains. At Boonsboro, Luray, and Grottoes we visited Civilian Public Service (cps) camps. They all had long dormitories with single beds running along each side and an aisle of beds in the center.

Someone at the Grottoes camp took us and several other people to see the Skyline Drive, which was quite new at the time. Little did I know that later in life, I would live three miles from Grottoes for nearly twenty years and raise a family there. Going back home, we visited at least one cps camp in Pennsylvania. I remember the Pennsylvania Turnpike as a topic of interest to my father. Going through a tunnel for the first time was a scary experience. On the return trip we had a several hour wait in Pittsburgh. We used this wait to visit a museum. I still recollect some of the exhibits, especially one including wax figures of Indians.

Visits to Grandmother and Aunt Mary Ann are recalled as early as 1941 and 1942. The Sears Roebuck & Co. catalog served as a booster seat at their table. I liked when Grandmother rocked me on her lap beside the wood-and-coal stove. A trip on a bobsled to Grandmother's house on a cold Christmas Day in 1944 was one of the highlights of my childhood. It was a cold morning with fresh snow on the ground. It was quiet—all you could hear was the light patter of the horses' hooves and an occasional squeak from the leather harnesses and the bobsled runners. We passed Johnson, Cunningham, and Boontown Schools. At the top of the hills we got on our sleds and coasted to the bottom. When the bobsled caught up, we jumped on, hooked our sleds to the back, and waited for the next hill. When our feet got cold there were hot, flat stones wrapped in a blanket to warm them. The stones were heated in the oven at home before we left. When we arrived, there were uncles, aunts, and cousins to greet us. The day was spent visiting and playing. Food and candy were plentiful.

Our parents tried to teach us the meaning of Christmas. Even so, going through the catalogs with our wishing and pretending games is probably what I remember best. The Sears Christmas catalog was the delight of our lives each holiday season. On Christmas Eve, we each set a plate at the kitchen table. The plate was placed at our regular position for meals. Our table was a busy place. In the peak years, we had eleven people at the table three times a day. On Christmas morning, we would usually find a bag of candy, an orange or other treasured fruit, and several toys on our plate. One Christmas, I went to sleep at the top of the stairs waiting for my parents to get up. A farm animal and building set, a windup train set, map games, and various coloring books are recalled as Christmas gifts of the past.

From a toddler on up, the day-to-day events unfolded before us in a consistent way. Along the way we were integrated into a chore and work routine for our family. I recall literally

having the hatchet passed to me at about age seven or eight. Mother asked me if I would kill a rooster for her. It involved going to the chicken house and catching it first. I had been instructed many times by observing others doing it. It wasn't a big deal. I was glad to be considered responsible enough. The chicken hook for catching, the chicken block to hold the head, and the hatchet to do the job, were the essentials. Learning to hold the legs, with wings tucked in with one hand, was sort of an art. If you didn't accomplish this you couldn't hold the rooster still enough to swing the hatchet. After the bleeding was completed, Mother held the carcass in boiling water long enough to scald it. Next, the feathers were plucked. The feather stubble was then singed by passing the plucked chicken over an open fire. This gave off a distinct, but not unpleasant, odor. Once exposed to it, you remember it the rest of your life.

Another early chore was walking barefooted behind Father on a horse drawn cultivator. This job involved uncovering small corn plants covered up by the cultivator plows. Since the three oldest were boys, we also got involved in some household chores. This only lasted until the girls were old enough to help. I don't recall doing dishes very often, but I frequently had to take my turn setting the table, churning butter, and carrying out garbage.

Fish, fruit, and produce peddlers were regulars at our house in the '40s. Only occasionally were there tramps. Tramp stories of the '30s were exciting topics of discussion on visits. For many years, jumping a freight train was high on a list of things I wanted to do. I recall that some of the peddlers were Jews with whom Father liked to visit. Stories of their lives in the old country interested him. Occasionally, Orthodox Jews from the city would come looking for animals suitable to kill for one of their Jewish holidays. My parents understood the need for balanced

meals which included all the food groups. Scurvy, we understood, came from an inadequate intake of vitamin C. In the wintertime, fruit and fruit juices were a staple in our daily diet. Mona Dave, our neighbor was very bow-legged from rickets. Father explained that the reason for this was a lack of vitamin D during his childhood.

During these summers, my brothers and I all helped drive hay wagons to pick up hay. A push or web loader was pulled behind the wagon. We first did this at Pifer Jakes. Controlling a large team seemed like a hard job at first. We were probably six or seven years old when we first did this. One of the adults would drive the loaded wagon to the barn. Once in the barn we drove a different team to pull the hay from the wagon to the mow. This was done with a rope and pulley system—hooked to a harpoon, or hay hooks. After Grandmother died, one of our uncles farmed the home place near Mount Hope. On one occasion there, on the way to the barn, a whole load of hay slid off the wagon. My uncle and I stayed on top and slid off with the hay. I remember feeling quite big when I related this to the others at home.

It seemed like only a year or two later we were plowing and disking with three and four horse teams. It wasn't until I was in the seventh grade that I could, by standing on a box, harness a full grown draft horse by myself. Two jobs not looked forward to were pulling wild mustard and hoeing corn. Digging post holes by hand was a very strenuous job.

All of us, including my sisters, shared in the milking. We would all start with one cow, the one that milked the easiest, and gradually increase to milking three or four as we became young teenagers. Certain cows had to be hobbled so they couldn't kick. Some would start releasing milk as soon as the udder and teats were washed. The cows were milked twice a day and as close to

twelve hours apart as we could make it. Our milk was shipped in ten-gallon cans. Right from the milking pail, the milk was poured into milk strainers set on top of the cans. Afterwards the cans were set into the milk trough for cooling. Cold well or spring water was run through the trough to cool the milk. Each community had its milk truck pickup routes every morning. The milk truck was often used to send messages to other farms. Our milk went to the Lawson Dairy in Akron, Ohio.

Even though competition, as a rule, was frowned on in the Amish community, in certain areas it seemed to be tolerated. We took a lot of pride in our dairy herd's production records. By testing through the Dairy Herd Improvement Program we could compare our herd with the top herds in the county. Most of the time our herd's average was competitive with the better herds. Occasionally we had the top herd. Milking by hand from early youth, I am told by friends, gives one a distinct handshake. As an adult, I had to tone down my grip when friends complained that their hand would never be the same.

Each spring Father rented pasture land for our heifers from his uncle who lived about six miles west of our place. This was an exciting adventure for us. We drove the fifteen to twenty head of cattle to the pasture. We kept them on the road by guarding driveways, yards, unfenced land, and crossroads while on horseback. As soon as the cattle passed one opening, we galloped ahead to block off the next one. We had one railroad crossing at the foot of a steep hill that created some apprehension on our part, but we never had to deal with an oncoming train during the drives. A buggy or hack with two people, serving as the cattle drivers, brought up the rear.

Taking horses to the blacksmith shop was a responsibility given to us by age nine or ten. We often rode or led the draft horses and drove the buggy horses. First the blacksmith

removed the old shoes and trimmed the hooves. We were allowed to operate the forge bellows that forced air through the coals to keep them red hot. While doing this, we watched the blacksmith heat the shoes red hot before starting the shaping and fitting on the anvil. Next came the hissing smoke with its distinct odor, when the hot shoes were applied to the hooves to check for fit. This was followed with additional hoof trimming and shoe shaping changes. When the fitting for all four shoes was completed, the shoes were dipped in cold water, giving off a cloud of steam. Lastly, the shoes were nailed on, the nails crimped, and the final fitting done with a hoof rasp.

Visits to the harness shop several times a year for harness and shoe repairs were another interesting chore. A single drive shaft ran the length of the harness shop. Six or eight different machines that were used for sewing and working with leather were connected to the shaft by belt and pulley. Watching the harness maker using his stick to connect and disconnect the belts to each machine as it was needed was enchanting. A diesel engine sitting outside the building provided the power. In prior years water power was used. The blacksmith, harness, and buggy shops all had their distinctive smells.

At Johnson School, Faye Thompson was our teacher. She taught all eight grades in one room. The floor of the schoolhouse had a dark oily finish. A majority of students went barefoot during the warm months. Each day we left with feet just about as black as you could make them. This called for a foot check before going to bed. Mentioning black also reminds me of the coal bin and furnace that kept the schoolhouse warm. During the winter, one of the older students came to school early to fire the furnace. On severely cold days during the winter, the older grades played "Monopoly" on the furnace room floor in the basement. The money, cards, and board were homemade.

Johnson School

I did have a trying experience the second day of school in the first grade. All summer my brothers had instructed me in the proper procedure for getting permission from the teacher to go to the outdoor toilet. Somehow, the first time I needed to go, my mind went into neutral. I became unsure of myself and panic set in. To this day, I can still feel that warm, wet sensation running down my leg and into my shoes. Mona Dave's Ada, an eighth grade neighbor girl, discovered my plight. Ada was one of our strawberry pickers during the summer. Ada got the teacher's attention and took me outside to dry my shoes and pants the best she could. She walked to and from school with me the next several days. She did it under the pretext of teaching me English, but was really protecting me from teasing. David Miller was Mona Dave's real name.

Driving by "Beeply" Christ Yoder's old place recently stirred some memories. "Beeply" Christ operated the local buggy shop for the Amish community. Of all things, the taste of delicious grape pie and homemade bread came to mind as I drove by. The Yoders had a large family. Their son Benjamin was in the first grade at Johnson School with me. I occasionally traded a peanut butter-and-jelly or bolongna sandwich with him for one of his homemade bread sandwiches or a piece of grape pie. The Sterling, and later, Nickles bakery truck delivered bread to our house twice weekly. The Yoder children considered the "bought bread" we got from the bread-man to be a delicacy.

For the first four decades of the 20th century, Amish children attended the small one room public schools that dotted the countryside. In Ohio, the consolidation of these schools into large schools was the start of Amish children losing their traditional way of education. Compulsory attendance laws requiring all children to stay in school until the age of sixteen was what actually led to the first Amish school being built. I recall when several Amish fathers from our community were put in jail for removing their children from school before they were sixteen.

One of the first of these schools was built at Fountain Nook in Wayne County. My father was on the school board which was made up of Amish men from the community. From the second grade on, this was the school we attended until we moved to another Amish community west of Holmesville. We had a two mile walk, morning and evening, during the five years we attended there. Milking, feeding the cattle, and taking care of the chickens were the main chores that had to be completed before school. To accomplish this, we needed to be in the barn by six o'clock. On stormy days involving rain, snow, or extreme cold, Father drove us to school with Ted in the buggy or sleigh.

Fountain Nook School

The first years we went to Fountain Nook School we got a nickel per week for spending money at Mert's store. Later this was increased to a dime. The memories of pondering over these nickels and dimes are pleasant indeed. Should it be spent early or late in the week, and will it be an ice cream bar, a candy bar, or a bottle of pop this week? On the walk home from school, the pace over the last half mile always increased. A snack and short rest period awaited us before chore time.

It always seemed to me that students learn as much from the grades above them as from their own lessons. The classes which were reciting in the front of the room and the students doing work on the blackboard could be observed by the rest of the students. We were encouraged to observe other students reciting and working on the blackboard if our own lessons were completed. Students who were adept at a given topic were often asked to help some of the younger students who were having problems. Outdoor games at school included Gray Wolf, Red Rover, Blackman, and Prisoners' Base. In wintertime, we played Fox-and-Geese when there was enough snow. In milder weather—in the spring and fall—softball was the favorite game for the older grades. I completed the end of the sixth and the seventh and eighth grades in the public school system after we moved west of Holmesville. I was thirteen at the time, and that was the extent of my formal education until after my twenty-sixth birthday.

From the earliest, I can remember we had Coleman gas lanterns for our main lights. They were used for doing the chores and any late outside work in the barn, chicken house, or in the mill. When less light was needed, we used kerosene lamps. The ones with mantles gave considerably more light than the ones with wicks only. Most of my early reading was done during winter evenings by the light of a kerosene lamp. Oil lanterns with red reflectors were hung on the side of the buggy for night driving. After we moved and had natural gas, piped gas was the source of illumination in the house. My mother still has this form of lighting.

On cold nights we often sat around the stove listening to stories read out loud to us. From a toddler up, stories read or recited were a regular part of our lives. Jack and the Beanstalk, The Three Bears, The Three Little Pigs, and Peter Rabbit were stories I recall being read to me. My mother and aunts mostly read the stories. In the early grades, these and Bible stories became our first recreational reading. From this, our reading went on to include *Lassie Come Home, Black Beauty*, and *Robinson Crusoe*. Other books we read were *The Swiss Family Robinson, Robin Hood*, and *The Adventures of Tom Sawyer. Uncle*

Tom's Cabin was read to us at school. I remember in the early '40s, Aunt Mary Ann telling Mother about a book she was reading. It was my introduction to Southern history, including the Civil War. The book was *Gone With the Wind*.

We worked in the truck patch a lot during the spring and summer. This was the big garden where potatoes, corn, tomatoes, squash, and melons were grown. It also included our raspberry patch. Radishes, carrots, lettuce, and other small produce, along with flowers, were grown in the small garden which was closer to the house. Summer and fall was also the time when all the canning was done. During the peak years when we were all at home, as many as a thousand pint, quart, and two-quart jars were canned in one season. Our basement shelves were filled to the brim with all kinds of fruits, vegetables, vegetable soup, and several kinds of meats. The grape arbors were separate from the orchard and garden. In the orchard, we had peach, apple, and pear trees. We had an outside oven to dry fruit. To my recollection this was only used for drying apples. Dried apple slices were called *schnitz*, the makings for *schnitz* pie.

Cider making time came in the fall and was an anticipated event. Cider apples were usually seconds that had fallen off the trees or were flawed in some other way. We filled bushel baskets with the apples. We used a one-horse hack, or spring wagon, to take a load to David Yoder's cider press. David was a farmer who did pressing work as a side business. His presses were operated with a steam engine. He was known to everyone as Cane Dave. My brothers and sisters first became acquainted with Cane Dave through his daughter Rebecca. She was, as we called her, our "hired girl" one summer. We knew her as Becky. She had a lively spirit and could run faster and jump higher than anyone we knew.

Cane Dave came by his name through another service he

provided for the community. He had a cane press for making molasses for those who raised corn sorghum for that purpose. Steam from the engine was piped through coils to the syrup holding vats where the syrup was boiled to a molasses grade. One year, when we took a load of apples to make cider, I watched the cane pressing process. We had to leave the apples with Cane Dave because it happened to be a cane pressing day. Cider was only made on Tuesdays and Thursdays that year. On Monday, Wednesday, Friday, and Saturday until noon, Cane Dave operated the cane press. We got to taste the syrupy product. It had its own distinct sweetness. To my recollection, we raised cane for molasses only one year.

During the war years when sugar was rationed many farm people used cane molasses for baking and cooking. Corn sorghum was raised much like field corn. At the proper stage, it was cut by hand with a corn knife. After the leaves were stripped and the tops cut off, the stalks were tied in bundles and hauled to the press. One year in the early '40s, Cane Dave operated the cane press and boiled syrup day and night from mid-September to mid-November, with the exception of Saturday afternoon and Sundays. Rebecca's sister told me recently that she and her sisters were introduced to store-bought breakfast cereals during these night shifts. Those that volunteered for the night work were treated to Post Toasties for the midnight break.

The cider and cane pressing bring to mind another fall rite—applebutter making. This followed cider pressing since cider was one of the ingredients for making applebutter. Usually a group of neighbors, relatives, or other friends got together for an *apple schnitzing* an evening or two before. At these get-togethers, the apples were washed, peeled, and quartered. The following day, a large copper kettle was filled with cider, the sliced apples, and sugar. The kettle hung on a beam between two posts. A large wood fire kept the kettle boiling. A tool with a handle about six feet long and with a paddle on one end that had one inch holes was used to stir the mixture. This kept the ingredients from burning and the kettle from scorching. The last ingredients, the spices, were added after the mixture took on an applebutter consistency. Applebuttering day only ended after those participating had tasted and proclaimed on the merits of the finished product. We often had "*schmere case und lotvike*" (cottage cheese and applebutter) at meals after applebuttering.

One year we gathered maple sugar sap. I had the job of tapping the maple trees with a hand auger and drill bit. It was embarrassing when one of my brothers discovered I had tapped an oak tree. Each day, the pails were emptied into a larger container that we hauled to the boiling vat. That year, after boiling, we had six gallons of maple syrup.

As young grade school children from seven to ten years of age, my brothers and I would occasionally take our horse and buggy to Grandmother's house on weekends. It was a six mile trip that took from thirty to forty-five minutes. On one occasion, on our way to a cousin's house, our horse was scared by a motorcycle and the buggy upset. When we went longer distances for visits as a family, we used two horses in the surrey. Ted and Queen furnished the horsepower for these journeys. The surrey was similar to our top covered buggy except it had two seats.

Sitting behind the seat on the buggy with our bare feet dangling out the back was a frequent way of travel. We often went to the Kidron livestock auction on Thursdays during the summer in this manner. Father gave us a nickel for spending money on these Thursday trips. On special occasions we got a dime. For a nickel, we had the choice of an ice cream cone, a bottle of soda pop, or a candy bar. Sale days at Kidron nearly always brought

several school friends to spend the day with. There were usually fruit and produce peddlers selling their goods off the back of their trucks. It wasn't unusual to have patent medicines being sold by fast talking sidewalk hawkers. One I recall was an Indian who fit the role of a true "snake-oil salesman." He got the people's attention by handling rattlesnakes that he kept in a wire cage. When he had the attention of a sufficient crowd, he switched to selling patent medicines. At the time, I had three brothers to alternate with on these Kidron trips. Often two of us went together. Sometimes we went with Grandfather. Going away in an automobile was also a greatly anticipated event.

The road in front of our house at the crossroads got extremely dusty during the summer. Each year, Father would get several barrels of used motor oil to apply to the road surface. An old five gallon bucket with holes punched in the bottom with spikes served as the applicator. The oil was applied at a slow jog while swinging the bucket to control the spray. The hired hand kept Father's spray bucket filled on the move. Several weeks after the oil application, the road was nearly as smooth as a paved one. I remember several uncles, and one older first cousin, racing barefoot on the road on Sunday afternoons. On hot days, the road surface was too hot to walk on barefoot. This brings to mind the lane to the strawberry patch. It was covered with several inches of warm fine dust that floated up between your toes and covered your feet. The dust remained warm overnight even on cool mornings. I remember dawdling when going after the cows on cool early mornings. Leaving the dusty lane was like leaving a warm mesmerizing shower.

There was a second way to warm your feet when going after the cows. Just at dawn, the cows were often still bedded down chewing the cud. On cool dewy mornings, after locating and rousing them, a steamy vapor often rose from their grassy beds.

Standing in your bare feet in these warm vacated beds was a pleasant reprieve from the cold wet grass.

Attending the new private Amish school from the second grade to the sixth grade entailed a two mile walk morning and evening. I don't recall ever disliking any of my teachers. Jesse Kindig was the first teacher at Fountain Nook School. We knew our parents would side with the teacher if we got into any trouble at school. Because of this, school problems were minimal. We did have an incident with the students of several of the families still going to Johnson School.

My oldest brother, Roy, made a booklet displaying birds during his fourth grade year. It won a prize and was hung in the front of the room on display for the students and visitors for a number of weeks. When it was taken down Roy took it home. On the way home we met the students from Johnson School. Dan and I, in the third and second grades respectively, were proud of Roy's booklet. We apparently brought the booklet to the attention of the other students by our demeanor. A scuffle ensued when Roy tried to keep them from seeing and/or getting their hands on the booklet. Roy fell with one of the others falling on top of him. This got me excited enough to hit the boy whom I thought was the offender over the head with my dinner bucket. He promptly collapsed in the roadside ditch. With this, my other brother Dan, cried out, "You killed him!" and the three of us took off running for home.

This was a grave crisis for a second grader in my setting. Physically harming, let alone killing someone, was not acceptable under any circumstances. No sin was considered as bad as killing. It was one of the most miserable nights of my life. A mountain was lifted off my chest when the supposedly mortally wounded one was found walking to school the next day. My indiscretion was paid for with several nights of bad dreams. We also walked to school through woods, brush, and fields for several weeks to avoid the other students. This also circumvented having to walk past the victim's home. The incident was forgotten and friendships reformed before our family moved to a larger farm where there was more work for the Weaver boys.

I recall Pearl Harbor Day and serious visits Father had with neighbors on the days following. The newspapers and neighbors were our sources of information about the war. As the war progressed, rationing coupons for gas, kerosene, shoes, meat, butter, and sugar became a part of life. Many of the young men we knew were drafted. Several neighbor boys enlisted in the military service. One day several women stopped along the road close to our house. They went to my father claiming they were out of gas. It was illegal to sell gas. They were so insistent that Father became suspicious they were faking being out of gas. He went to the car with them. When they pretended ignorance to his questions, he, to their surprise, got into the car and started it. Once their ruse was uncovered, they drove away in a huff.

From listening to the adults discuss the war, we realized the serious nature of the conflict. For a long time after the war began, my brothers and I were afraid when large airplanes flew over the farm. Soon Roy, followed several years later by Dan and me, developed the ability to read the daily newspapers. Our paternal grandparents, living across the road, got the *Wooster Daily Record*. We got the *Cleveland Plain Dealer*. Signs of the war could be seen locally. Many times, large numbers of airplanes would practice dogfights in the sky above us. They were trainers, I believe, from the Great Lakes Naval Station. Blimps from their hangars in Akron frequently flew over our home.

Newspapers supplemented the eight years of school that formed the basic education for most of the young Amish men and women I grew up with. News that I recall being newsworthy enough for discussion included; events of the war and its end in the mid '40s, President Roosevelt's death, the Truman-Dewey election, reconstruction in Europe, the Nuremberg trials, Joseph Stalin and communism, and the start of the United Nations. A Joe Louis fight, the 1946 Red Sox, and the 1948 and 1954 Indians winning the pennant are remembered. I experienced seeing baseball players like Ted Williams, Bob Feller, and Mickey Mantle in games at Cleveland in the '50s. From the '50s I recall the Korean War, Eisenhower being elected president, the Alger Hiss trial, the Sam Sheppard trial, and the announcement by the Eisenhower administration that an interstate highway system would be built. The McCarthy and Kefauver hearings and the Suez Canal War are also remembered from the '50s. The beginning of the race into outer space with the Russians orbiting the earth with Sputnik in 1957 was long a topic of discussion.

As a boy under the age of ten, several events that I recall left me with a lifelong impact. A sister, Amanda, was born in May 1942. She had a type of heart defect called blue-baby, a defect that is routinely repaired today. She died in February 1943. I recall my mother crying when she realized Amanda was dying. Mother sent me to the chicken house to get Father. After Amanda died, Mona Dave Tina helped us put a penny on each of her eyes. This, we were told, would properly close them in death. The death of my grandmother, Amanda Yoder Schlabach, in February 1944, left a lasting impression. The accidental carbon monoxide poisoning deaths of two of Father's first cousins and a third young Amish boy in March 1946, left me thinking for weeks about the finality of death. Funerals, like church services, were held in the house or barn depending on the season and weather. Because of the way it affected the adults I was around, the suicide of a mentally handicapped young Amish man dampened my spirits for a long time.

The polio epidemic in the '50s was a sobering experience. The summer the epidemic peaked, public meetings, including church services, were canceled for a period of time. As the summer went on, new cases of polio in the Amish community were reported on a near weekly basis.

On a different note, I recall lying in our yard at night looking at the stars and thinking about time and space having no end. I wondered what would happen if you traveled in a straight line straight up from the earth's surface at a million miles a second for a million years. What would you hit? What was on the other side if you hit something? Can time stop? Would time stop if the last person on earth died? The answer from my parents, that God is, and always was everywhere, still seems like the best acceptable answer.

Oral Family History

AN ACTIVITY WE ALL ENJOYED WAS THE RETELLING OF STO-ries handed down through our family. These were often captivating to us. Mother related stories her grandfather told her of his boyhood days. Mother kept house and cooked for him in 1926 after Great-grandmother's death. One fall, Great-grandfather and an older brother were in the woods of their Somerset County, Pennsylvania, home picking up hickory nuts. One of them looked up to discover a panther stalking them. He was creeping along the top of a rail fence towards them a short distance away. The cat was black and had a long tail slowly wagging from side to side. The boys dropped their bag and raced home. Their father went back with a gun, but couldn't find the panther. He did recover their bag of nuts and the boys' mittens which they had left when they ran. At the end of this story we were always reminded that our great-grandfather Abraham Yoder was the little boy and that Samuel Yoder, our great-great-grandfather was the little boy's father.

This same great-grandfather, Abraham Yoder, told Mother of hearing Civil War cannons near their home as a five year old. When Abraham was twelve years old, his family moved from Somerset County, Pennsylvania, to Holmes County, Ohio. Abraham and his two oldest brothers brought their team and wagon. It's likely they brought other livestock in addition to farm tools and household goods. They crossed a large stream or river at a ford late one afternoon. Several of the boys rode the horses pulling the wagon. After crossing to the other side, they went only a few miles farther before camping for the night. The next morning one of the mares in the wagon hitch was missing. After searching for some time, they found her with a new foal. This caused a change in travel plans—they now had to wait until the new baby was strong enough to trot alongside its mother to Holmes County. This reminds me of my own childhood, when it wasn't unusual to see a mare and a buggy go by on the road with a little foal trotting alongside. Because of traffic dangers, one doesn't see this anymore.

In later years, Great-grandfather Abraham's sister Amanda, who was a year older than he, told several of her grand-nieces about the rest of the family's trip by train. When the train arrived in what she thought was Zanesville, Ohio, their father, Samuel, went to get someone to take the family and their belongings the rest of the way to Holmes County. Amanda, who was fourteen, and her mother stayed outside the train station with their baggage. While they waited, the three smaller children, Mary, Caroline, and Jonas, became fussy. The younger ones cried from being tired and thirsty. When a man came by and offered her mother and the children water and a place to rest if they went with him, she accepted the offer. She promptly changed her mind when the man went down an alley and started up a long outside stairway. She remembered that she had all the family's money sewed in the hem of her dress and realized that no one was watching the baggage. They returned to their baggage and found it undisturbed. In later years, Jonas, the baby mentioned in the story above, had his appendix removed at home on their kitchen table. His wife held a kerosene lamp for light during the operation. Jonas and his wife described this event to my father.

Nine years after arriving in Holmes County, young Abraham married Mattie Oswald. He told my mother he wanted Mattie for his wife the first time he met her. Since she was only thirteen, he had to wait several years. He described their wedding and the small log cabin in which they lived. In the evenings he would split wood outside a window while she sat knitting inside. They used a candle on the window sill for their light. Three years after they were married he was ordained a minister. Thirty years later, the lot fell on him again, and he was ordained an Amish bishop. We have several letters written to the elderly Abraham after the death of his wife Mattie in 1926. They were sent by two of his cousins, Leah and Fannie Beachy, from Aurora, West Virginia. These letters were written at the time my mother, as a young teenager, kept house and cooked for her recently widowed grandfather.

Another story involving ancestors was the Berks County, Pennsylvania, Indian massacre. It involved the Jacob Hochstetler family, in 1757, during the French and Indian War. One dark evening, after a young folks' gathering at the Hochstetler cabin, their dog's bark alerted them to the presence of Indians. They managed to get the door closed before the Indians got in, but in doing so, Jacob Junior suffered a gunshot wound to his leg. When the family wouldn't let the Indians in, they set fire to the cabin. Two of the sons begged their father to let them shoot at the Indians, but he steadfastly refused. He told them, "It is not right to take the life of another, even to save one's own." The father, Jacob, and his two oldest sons were good marksmen, but the father's wishes prevailed.

When the fire intensified, the family went to the basement. There they kept the fire from burning through the floor by sprinkling cider on the ceiling. The winter's cider supply was kept in barrels in the basement. As dawn appeared they observed the Indians leaving. When they deemed it safe, they started to come out through a small basement opening. A young Indian lagging behind in the orchard to pick up ripe peaches saw them and gave the alarm. They were immediately surrounded. Joseph got away by outrunning two Indians. After getting away, he hid. Unbeknownst to him, one of the Indians saw his hiding place. At the cabin, the mother, Barbara; the injured son, Jacob Junior; and a daughter were killed by the Indians. Jacob and his son Christian were taken captive. When the Indians left, they surrounded Joseph's hiding place and took him captive, too.

Over the next few years the three captives were at various times in Ohio, Michigan, New York, and Pennsylvania. They were thought to have been in Detroit, Michigan, and Erie, Pennsylvania, for short periods during their captivity. Jacob, the father, managed to escape from the Indians in 1760. Through treaties, one of the boys is thought to have been released in 1763 and the other one in 1764. The exact dates of the father's escape and the sons' releases are not established for certain. Jacob is thought to have made his escape from somewhere in northeastern Ohio. At least one of the sons was released to General Bouquet in Coshocton. For as long as I can remember, my lineage as a direct descendant of this Jacob Hochstetler through his daughter Barbara, was drawn out for me.*

*See *Descendants of Jacob Hochstetler* for more details, pages 29 through 45.

Oral family history and legal records agree that the Weaver family immigrant was Jacob Weaver, who arrived in Philadelphia on the ship *King of Prussia* in October, 1764. He and a cousin, Christian, came down the Rhine River to Rotterdam where they embarked for America via London. Jacob was sixteen years old when he arrived in Philadelphia. He was born in 1748 in Zurich, Switzerland. According to oral family history, he and his brother were sold as indentured servants to pay for their passage. Legal records show they ended up in Berks County, Pennsylvania. It hasn't been established whether or not they served their indentured years there or went there afterwards. Both of them served in the Revolutionary War.

Historical information from that time shows many Mennonite and Brethren farmers were given orders to provide a team and wagon for Washington's Army of the Delaware. The order included a provision for getting their teams back if they provided a driver. The pacifist Quakers, Mennonites, Brethren, and Amish apparently unwillingly provided help for Washington's crossing of the Delaware during the Valley Forge winter. Whether Jacob served in this capacity, or as a combatant, has not been determined. After the war, Jacob moved from Berks County to Lancaster County, Pennsylvania. There he married Magdalena, a daughter of Jacob Oberholtzer of Brecknock Township. Their first son, Christian, was born there. Later, Jacob was one of the early settlers in Somerset County, Pennsylvania. From all indications, he never accepted a land grant for two thousand acres that was offered him for his military service.

Oral tradition says that three of Jacob Weaver's sons came from their Somerset County, Pennsylvania home to Holmes County, Ohio, in 1811. They are thought to have walked and driven their cattle ahead of them. It is likely they came up the Williamson Trail to the crossing on the Tuscarawas River.

Samuel, one of the brothers, staked a claim in the Walnut Creek Valley just south of present day Walnut Creek, Ohio. He is our family's direct ancestor. By 1815, he had proven his claim and received a title to the land. The Williamson Trail was named after an infamous man of that name who led the massacre of Christian Indians at Gnadenhutten on March 8, 1782. On the occasion of the massacre, his party came up this trail from Wheeling, West Virginia. The restored buildings and grounds of the sister settlement Schoenbrunn Moravian Mission, are located southeast of present day New Philadelphia, Ohio.*

William Henry Harrison having defeated the Indians under Tecumseh in the battle of Tippecanoe in 1811, made the opening of the Ohio and Indiana Territory safe for settlers. Our ancestors were a part of the initial fifteen to twenty families in the Walnut Creek Amish settlement. This settlement, like the other new settlements in Ohio, got involved indirectly in the War of 1812 when William Hull, Governor of the Michigan territory, surrendered Detroit to the British. With this surrender, many of the settlers west of New Philadelphia became alarmed and headed for the Tuscarawas River ferry at Dover, Ohio. They were afraid the Indians, with British support, would invade Ohio. These people congregated at New Philadelphia, the new county seat for Tuscarawas County. Some of the families stayed on the other side of the river, while others went back to Pennsylvania. Still others returned to work their land claims, leaving the women and children on the east side of the river.

Samuel's son Peter homesteaded on the next ridge north of Chestnut Ridge. This was approximately four miles northwest of the Samuel Weaver homestead. The ridge Peter settled on is still called Weaver's Ridge. A letter written by my great-great-grandfather Benjamin Weaver, Peter's son, was found in a family Bible. In it, Benjamin says,

*See, *That Dark and Bloody River* by Allan W. Eckert, pages 315 through 318.

"Soon after the Indian scare came ... most of them [the Amish settlers] went back again to Pennsylvania and stayed several years again and some of them only went part of the way back ... during the war of 1812."

He goes on to say,

"A company of soldiers came through here from Toledo, commanded by Col. Fred Hoff formerly a native of [sic] Summersett County, Pennsylvania. They took up their quarters and lodged at the residence of Abraham Gerber and Jonas Miller at Walnut Creek and with same more events could be named."

This letter was written to M. Joseph Steiner of Columbus Grove, Putnam County, Ohio, on August 8, 1902. Benjamin's sources were likely his father, Peter, and his grandfather Samuel.

The immigrant Jacob Weaver's son was Samuel Weaver. Samuel's son was Peter Weaver. Peter's son was Benjamin Weaver. Benjamin's son was Emanuel Weaver. Emanuel's son was Atlee Weaver. Atlee's son was Monroe Weaver, and Monroe was my father. My father remembered visiting his great-grand-father Benjamin and spending time with him. He went visiting with him in his buggy. Benjamin, quoted above, was born in 1838 and died in 1919. My father remembered his death and attended his funeral as a ten-year-old boy. I recall visits to Great-grandfather Emanuel's home. I recall him holding and rocking me in his hickory rocker. I attended his funeral as a boy of ten. He was born in 1864 and died in 1948 at age eighty-four.*

My great-grandmother on my father's maternal side, Barbara Yoder, came to Ohio as a teenager in the early 1870's. As the story goes, there was a church division in their Somerset County, Pennsylvania, Amish community. Barbara's boyfriend and his family belonged to the more liberal branch of the divided church. In order to get the two separated, Barbara's father

*See, family number 12446 in, *Descendants of Barbara Hochstetler and Christian Stutzman*, page 829.

sent her to live with relatives in Ohio. Her older brother Christian came with her by Conestoga wagon. Barbara married Isaac Wengerd several years after arriving. Christian married a woman also named Barbara, who was the daughter of John and Fannie Hostetler Yoder, of Shanesville. The old John Yoder home is still standing in what is now Sugarcreek, Ohio. The house was moved from its original site very recently against the wishes of local historians. My great-grandmother and her brother came to Ohio on a freight wagon owned and operated by a local Amish man, Jacob Esch, from the Johnstown, Pennsylvania area. The wagon was later bought at the Esch family auction by Barbara's brother, Levi. After years of family use it was stored in the Yoder family barn in 1931, where it is to this day.

The barn this wagon was stored in over the last sixty years is a little over a mile north of Davidsville, in Somerset County, Pennsylvania. The farm is just several miles north of the farm that the well-known NFL quarterback, Jeff Hostetler, lived on as a child. His father still lives there. Over the years, my sons and I have referred to him as cousin Jeff when friends were around. Recently, I found out that we are actually distant cousins.

The descendants of Christian and Barbara continued periodic contact with the Somerset relatives after their move to Ohio. Father recalled his grandmother, Barbara, telling of her childhood days in Pennsylvania and the wagon trip to Ohio. From the time Father was a small boy in grade school until he was an adult, he exchanged letters with one of his second cousins, Morgan Yoder. Later, through his father Levi, Morgan came into possession of the Conestoga wagon in which Great-grandmother Barbara came to Ohio. We are, at the time of this writing, arranging the restoration of this wagon in conjunction with Morgan's three daughters, Ruth, Martha, and Lois. The

Somerset County and Holmes County communities and descendants of Christian and Barbara are also involved in this project.

As it turned out, of the Yoders' ten children, the only ones that married Amish and have Amish descendants today were Barbara and Christian, who came to Ohio in the Conestoga wagon. Three of Christian's sons moved to the Arthur, Illinois, area around the turn of the century and have many Amish descendants there. One of Barbara's grandsons was Emanuel Mullet, a well-known businessman who lived in Holmes and Tuscarawas County, Ohio, all his life.

An intriguing mystery surrounds the life of one of my Great-uncles. Great-grandmother Barbara, one of the occupants of the Conestoga wagon, married Isaac Wengerd in 1881. The great-uncle referred to above was their firstborn child, Daniel. He died at age 23, three months before his sister Fannie, my grandmother, was married to Atlee Weaver, my grandfather. Father told me that Grandmother refused to talk about Dan, as they called him. In my experience as a child, and later as an adult, no one in the family seemed to know, or was willing to talk about Dan. A wall of silence appears to have surrounded Daniel's life and death.

Over the last ten years more information has become available through non-Amish members of the community, as well as through family members. Unfortunately, the last of Daniel's siblings died in 1989. Many of Daniel's nephews and nieces are still living, but none were born before he died. Information from them, and other older people in the community, has allowed me, in part, to piece together his short life. Additional information was obtained from The College of Wooster and two newspapers of that day. News of his death appeared in the *Wooster Democrat* on December 6, 1906 and in the *Canton Repository* on

December 4, 1906.

The problem appears to have started in his early teen years with his unwillingness to conform to the Amish way of life. Oral history from the sources mentioned above all agree in their description of Daniel as exceptionally intelligent and a good athlete. From information in the newspapers, he is known to have attended The College of Wooster and The Ohio State University in his late teens and/or early twenties. It was known to the family that he traveled a lot. His favorite means of travel appears to have been "jumping freight trains." Daniel taught school for at least two terms before his death. The schools that he is known to have taught at were in Boontown and Elm Grove. Both were one-room country schools in the Fredericksburg and Mount Hope area of Holmes County, Ohio.

The newspaper articles speculated that the cause of death was an injury he received in a football game about six weeks before his death. His team played the Canton Bulldogs, a semi-pro team, on October 8, 1906. There were no totally professional football teams in existence at that time. Football players of that day wore no protective gear. A detailed article in the *Canton Repository* described the game. Daniel played left guard. The newspaper article described Daniel's team as, "lighter rivals ... greatly outweighed on the line." The game was played at Lake Park in Canton, Ohio, with an estimated one thousand people in attendance. The article describing the game was in the October 8, 1906 *Repository*. This game was played over six weeks before his death. The semi-pro teams apparently used other local town teams to prepare for their more serious league rivals. The newspapers indicate that the Massillon Tigers played the Canton Bulldogs on November 29th, the day before Daniel's death. The newspapers played this game up as the game of the season. Daniel's Mount Hope friends said he was in Massillon that day. It would appear that he was more likely a spectator than a player.

Contrary to the newspaper articles, oral family history explains his death as having occurred from injuries he received when he jumped off a freight train in Fredericksburg. Friends of Daniel in Mount Hope, where he lived in a boarding house, said that he had a serious fall the night before his death. The accident occurred in Fredericksburg when he jumped off a freight train that was going too fast. George Inks, a friend of Daniel's who later was the Postmaster of Mount Hope, told friends that Daniel bicycled from Fredericksburg to Mount Hope after the accident late in the day of November 29th. George went on to say that Daniel was found dead in bed the next morning. An autopsy was done at the place of death, and death was determined to have been caused by a brain hemorrhage. Other potential sources of information are Daniel's school records from The Ohio State University and The College of Wooster, as well as from the public schools he taught in. The only photo of Daniel that the family knows about was given to one of his nieces by George Inks.

Father would also tell us stories of Texas. In November, 1924, he, with his parents, brothers and sisters, and several other families, boarded a private Pullman car in Cleveland, Ohio. It was the start of a fifteen-hundred mile trip to the southern tip of Texas, near LaFeria. They moved to a twenty acre produce and citrus fruit farm in the Rio Grande Valley. Some of the group also raised cotton. Father told us of a three hour delay in St. Louis which they spent at the St. Louis Zoo. At the zoo, Father's sister Ada got rid of some small pebbles that a friend had given her. She was carrying them in her pocket to prevent homesickness. She had felt silly carrying them, but later when she got homesick, she wished she had kept them. During the two years they lived in Texas, my father learned some Spanish from neighbors, friends, and their Mexican help. The settlement lacked a dependable marketing system for their fruit and produce. According to some, the real reason the settlement didn't survive was its lack of ministers and additional settlers, not its failure to survive financially.

My father told of a bootlegging incident involving the farm help. Father went with one of the hired Mexican workers for a ride in his old car. He drove towards the Rio Grande River until the road ended. They walked the rest of the way to the river. After the worker went down to the water's edge and whistled, a Mexican appeared out of the bushes on the other side, untied a little boat and rowed across. He gave the worker a package which contained a jug of whiskey. Father described the whiskey bearer as a fierce looking man. He realized that this was illegal since the incident took place during the time when the United States was in prohibition. He described himself as a scared sixteen-year-old boy who didn't make any more unauthorized trips to the river.

Father also told us of a trip to a horse sale in Lexington, Kentucky, with his cousin Emanuel Mullet. They went to buy standard bred race horses for resale as buggy horses to the Amish. The horses, for one reason or another, weren't good enough for the racetrack. The trip took place in 1932 during the Depression. They bought seven horses. On the way home they had several flat tires and ran out of money. With the help of a friendly stranger, they roused a garage owner. Before getting to the garage, they discussed whether to tell the man before or after the tire was fixed, that they had no money. They decided to tell him before. Emanuel ended up having to leave a jeweled pocket watch, a gift from his father, with the man for security. He returned the next day and got his watch back.

Young Teen Years

WHEN I WAS TWELVE, THE YEAR AFTER WE MOVED TO THE Holmesville community, we built a new barn and straw shed. All the framing lumber came from our woods. It was at a time when chain saws were first coming into popular use. The chain saw we used required two men to operate it. A sawmill was set up not far from the building site. Then the carpenter crew leader calculated the dimensions and quantities needed for the completion of the project. After this, the trees were cut and the logs were pulled from the woods to the sawmill site by team and tractor. The sawyer then used the lumber list to saw out the lumber needed. After the foundation was completed, the mason crews laid the concrete block walls. Next the sawed timbers and framing lumber were taken to the building site. Here they were arranged for the most efficient use of the volunteer help on barn-raising day.

On the morning of the barn raising, most of our neighbors,

in addition to many relatives and friends from farther away, came to help. Several loads of helpers from our former home community came by truck. Livestock trucks were used for this purpose. Many women came along to prepare the food for the day. An estimated four to five hundred men and boys helped with the work. By late in the day, we had a large new barn and straw shed. These buildings were the center of our farm work activities until each of us went on to pursue our life's work as adults.

School and church provided the friends for my growing-up years. Nearly all my friends had a favorite baseball team. Most were Cleveland Indians fans. Since an older boy I liked rooted for the Boston Red Sox, I became a Red Sox fan. I recall being very impressed when I found out that my father had seen the New York Yankees and Babe Ruth play in Cleveland. He had attended several Cleveland Indians games in the late '20s and early '30s. In the '50s, nearly all the major league teams played afternoon double-headers on Sundays and holidays. Because of the two-for-the-price-of-one advantage, the baseball games we attended were nearly all double-headers. We always aimed to be there before batting practice and we usually got at least one fly ball.

After mid-grade school, we got together with our friends nearly every Sunday afternoon. On church service Sundays, we got together after church. When weather permitted, we played softball or other outside games. Rook was a favorite card game for bad weather days. In my early teens, hunting and fishing became enjoyable pastimes, in season. Mushroom hunting was an anticipated springtime activity. In late April and early May, favorite mushroom sites were explored during field work when the horses rested.

About once a summer, the neighborhood got together and

hired a livestock hauler to clean out his truck and take us for a fishing trip to Tappan Lake, Pleasant Hill Lake, or one of the other larger water impoundments in the area. On these trips, a group of twenty or more would ride in the back of the truck. Standing on the side slats with friends, with hair blowing in the wind, was the preferred way of travel. We usually caught some fish, but for us the outing and the ride were just as important.

In 1949 or 1950, our neighbors, the Schmidheisers, got a television set. We were forbidden from accepting their invitation to come into their house to watch, but we were quite fascinated by the TV stories we heard in school. Over the next several years, I had occasion to watch some baseball games and several boxing matches at their house.

Most of my non-Amish friendships developed after we moved to the Holmesville community when I was eleven. Many were from the new school we attended in Big Prairie, Ohio. My first encounter with foul and profane language was an unanticipated and startling experience that occurred on the school bus. After having walked to school for six years, going to school on a bus was an unusual experience. I attended school in Big Prairie through the eighth grade.

My school discipline record was blemished in the seventh grade at Big Prairie. I wasn't considered a troublemaker, but hitting a girl sitting one row to the right and four seats ahead of me with a rubber band propelled paper-wad wasn't a good idea. Her short yelp got the teacher's attention. With a little prodding, the teacher soon had the culprit—me—identified. What I thought was a good student-teacher relationship quickly disappeared. The teacher had definite plans for a paper-wad free classroom.

My first and only experience with a wooden paddle ensued. It was applied hard enough to interfere with comfortable sitting

Author, age 11

for several days. As one might expect, I didn't think the crime deserved the punishment. Since I don't recall having had any further interest in the art of paper-wad shooting, I guess the paddling had its desired effect. It took several weeks for the news to filter back to my parents. They listened to my version of what happened and decided the matter had been adequately addressed.

In the summer of 1990, I was honored with a surprise invitation from Larry and Anna Mae Martin. The 1955 graduating class from Big Prairie High School invited me to their thirty-fifth class reunion. I had parted from the class after the eighth grade in 1951.

We had built a good-sized farm pond the year after we moved. It soon became a favorite local swimming hole on hot summer days. Many of our new friends from school became regulars at the pond.

On the Holmesville farm, we had a lot more work; both milking and general farm chores. Nell and Bell were the favorite team for heavy farm work. Ted was an all-purpose horse that worked well in the field, or as a buggy horse for the road. As the three oldest of us reached our late teens, we started working some at non-farm trades. My two oldest brothers learned the mason trade. I worked for my future brother-in-law, Homer Coblentz, who was a painting contractor. At first, this was only during the times when farm work was caught up. Later, it developed into full-time work for all of us. Farm work got tiresome, but only when much of the work had to be done alone.

Father claimed he could tell a lot about a person by watching him plow. A plow furrow that wasn't straight represented slothfulness to him. Plowing with a walking plow, with two or three horses, was something I enjoyed. This was especially so when Father, or one of my brothers, was also plowing. The

Oliver Company made the best walking plow. We calculated our speed with the walking plow at two miles an hour. With a plow that had a twelve inch shear point, two times the number of feet in a mile (5,280) was the number of square feet plowed in an hour. This came to about two acres being plowed in an eight-hour day. Allowing for the horses to rest, and not always plowing straight, one-and-one-half acres per day was a good day's work. At the end of a twelve mile day of walking in the soft soil of a plow furrow and wrestling the plow handles, one knew he had done a day's work. You could call it walking with a purpose.

Walking through a plowed field at just the right time after a rain occasionally produced an Indian arrowhead. One year, I found a nearly perfect tomahawk head.

In those days, there was no need to ride a stationary bicycle or walk up and down the road to stay in shape. To this day, I feel silly doing what to me subconsciously is purposeless walking. Even though I know it is healthy, those furtive over-my-shoulder glances are real. I wonder who is watching today. Am I shameless and without dignity? Absolutely not, but I refuse to swing my arms like a baton twirler while I'm walking.

During my teen years, a lot of work involved the whole family. Shocking wheat and oats and husking corn often included everyone over ten or eleven years of age. We husked corn by hand using two wagons. The youngest children sat in a corner of one of the wagons with a board across the corner to protect them from the thrown ears. Each wagon had four huskers who husked four rows each pass. In the early years when we were too young to help much, Father hired help to husk. The huskers were usually women. Since I've come back to Holmes County, I've seen a number of women as medical patients who reminded me they helped husk corn and pick strawberries for us when I was a small child. I've also seen several schoolmates from my first year at Johnson School as patients.

My mother had an inherent interest in nature which she passed on to us in varying degrees. I am speaking of the animals, birds, wildflowers, trees, and other life forms that everyone living and working on a farm encounters. I have regretted not learning more of this aspect of farm life when the opportunity was there. Some of my priorities were in the wrong place.

Our neighborhood young married men and teenage and older boys had horse races every week or two during several summers. We measured a mile stretch of straight and level dirt road for the course. The course ran south from Moorhead Church. Trotters and pacers raced together, two at a time. We used two-wheeled—what we called—road carts. This was later stopped when the church elders frowned on it. I enjoyed playing softball and baseball, and during my late teen years played for Mount Eaton in the Wayne County fast pitch league, and for Berlin (Ohio) in the Tri-County baseball league.

The winter I was eighteen, I worked for a veterinarian near Bath, outside of Akron, Ohio, for several months. One night another worker talked me into going with him for a workout at a downtown Akron gym. As it turned out, the workout was boxing. After several of these trips, I agreed to box a practice round one night. A sound thrashing by a younger, more experienced boxer perturbed me. Several weeks later, I agreed to regular workouts and entered the novice division in that year's Golden Glove tournament. I won the first bout and lost the second one. We were just at the end of the first round in the first bout when someone outside the ring stood up and yelled. The referee stepped between us. I had forgotten to take off my glasses. That was more embarrassing than losing the next fight.

My father was good with numbers and was especially interested in geography and history. We were all taught the states and capitals as pre-schoolers and early grade scholars. This was a topic of some fun during my two years of voluntary service, as you will see later. Father's attitude about school was—be serious and learn all you can. He also felt school beyond the eighth grade for farm boys was unnecessary. He expected us to do well in school and took some pride when we did, even though he went to some length to hide it. When I completed the eighth grade, I would have liked to continue on to high school, but I never could get myself to ask my parents. I am sure Father's honest response would have been not only to say no, but also to ask himself, "Where did I fail?"

I started dating in my mid to late teens. My cousin Dennis Schlabach had told me several years earlier about Lovina Coblentz, a nice girl in his class at Elm Grove School. I saw her the first time three years before our first date when we stopped at their place on our way home from the Kidron sale. Father bought a coon hound pup for us from her brother. From the back of the truck, I watched her shyly walk from the front yard to behind the house. I always appreciated Cousin Dennis' good judgment. Her parents were Andy and Emma Coblentz. Her ancestors, like mine, were Amish. The Coblentz family lived between Mount Hope and Fredericksburg, eleven miles from our place—four miles west of Holmesville.

The first several years Lovina and I dated, I drove to her parents' place in my buggy for part of nearly every weekend. Going home late at night, I frequently fell asleep but Sailor, my horse, knew the way home. His hooves would wake me when we came from a gravel road onto a blacktop road. When I was nineteen, I bought an old car that served for my transportation to ball games and other social events. My father and I reached a somewhat unspoken truce regarding the car. His position was, "No, I don't want you to have a car, but if you are honorable and trustworthy in your relationships, and work here at home, we'll just pretend the car isn't." With this, my car had a parking place in a corner of one of our fields as long as I had it.

In the early winter of 1956, I spent two months in Sarasota, Florida. Baseball connoisseurs will appreciate the baseball players I saw either in spring training or in regular season games that year. The roster included Hank Aaron, Frank Robinson, Willie Mays, Stan Musial, and Roberto Clemente from the National League. In the American League, I saw Mickey Mantle, Ted Williams, Al Kaline, and Larry Doby. Whitey Ford, Herb Score, and Early Wynn were pitchers I watched play that year. I saw Satchel Paige in Cleveland in the early '50s and Jackie Robinson in spring training in 1956.

Farm home as a youth, near Holmesville in Holmes County Ohio

Marriage and Voluntary Service

DURING THESE YEARS, MOST OF MY FRIENDS, ESPECIALLY those older than I, were either drafted by the Selective Service or they volunteered for service before they were drafted. As conscientious objectors to military service, they worked for two years as attendants and orderlies at general and psychiatric hospitals. In the fall of 1958, I signed up for two years of voluntary service at the Holmes County draft board in Millersburg, Ohio. By volunteering, I had some choice as to where I would work. Wooster Community Hospital was one of my choices. It was close to my wife-to-be and to my home. I had no special interest in medicine or hospitals at the time. I went because it was the alternative service opportunity our government provided. At the time I would probably have been offended had someone suggested that I had an interest in medicine.

To my surprise, I liked my work as an operating room orderly. My job included bringing surgical patients from the floor to the operating rooms and back. This, plus cleaning, getting supplies, and running other errands, took up most of the day. Less frequently, I was asked to help during surgery. I had to learn sterile technique and occasionally had to scrub-in to hold a retractor or a limb to be amputated. Later, as I gained some experience, Dr. Frank Cebul had me assist with lacerations and other injuries in the emergency room. Cleansing wounds, cutting sutures, and dressing wounds were the extent of my contributions.

One day, Dr. Cebul told me how in medical school days, he used to practice suturing. He took a grapefruit or orange and made his own lacerations. Closing these with stitches was good practice for learning suturing technique. After Dr. Cebul told me about practicing suturing, I started saving the opened unused sutures when I cleaned up the operating room at the end of the day. After a couple days of special favors to Pat Scott, the operating room supervisor, the next discarded needle holder found its way into my locker inside an envelope. With the needle holder and a bandage scissors, I soon became adept at suturing badly lacerated grapefruits and oranges. By slicing the fruit in two and carefully removing the edible part, I found a way to increase my proficiency. I turned the outside of the peeling in and practiced tying good stitches within the limited space. When I reached the point where I could place a tight suture inside a turned-in orange, I felt proficient. During the first year, I began wondering about some kind of work involving health care. The kind of relationship that developed with patients, even as an orderly, intrigued me. Even though I delighted in my work, the conflict with a traditional Amish life and education precluded me from pursuing it.

That spring, personal convictions led me to make a faith commitment to God and to the church. Subsequently, in the summer of 1959, I became a member of the church. Later that year, on October 15, 1959, Lovina and I were married. We had a traditional Amish wedding at Melvin Weavers. Mrs. Weaver was one of Lovina's aunts. They lived about a half mile east of Lovina's farm home. Andy Mast, the Amish bishop from my west Holmesville church district, performed the wedding ceremony. The meals and social functions were at Lovina's parents' home. We had a large wedding. Friends, neighbors, relatives, and a number of hospital employees attended. Dr. Charles and Dorothy Hart from Millersburg also attended. Three days after the wedding, we moved into what we thought was a nice apartment in Wooster. At the start of our marriage, I earned eighty-five cents an hour at the hospital. Lovina did housecleaning for the gentry of Wooster and earned from five to ten dollars a day. Our income was more than adequate for our needs. In October, 1960, our first child, David, was born. Also, in 1960, two of my wife's brothers' families changed their church membership from the Amish to the Beachy Amish. The following fall, we also made this change.

I enjoyed the work and relationships established during these two years. Once or so a week, we visited with others in our service unit. I read a lot during my days off. It took a while to get used to only an eight-hour workday. In my experience, one worked until the job was done or until daylight or the weather set the limits. Part-time odd jobs were sometimes available on our days off. At work, I was accused of hustling some of the nurses, orderlies, and aides. To the takers, I offered to pay a dollar if I couldn't name all fifty states in less than a minute. The timing was arranged to do it the first time in just under a minute. This was followed by giving the takers an opportunity to get their dollar back. I offered to pay back their dollar if I couldn't say all fifty states in less than thirty seconds. I didn't always get paid, but they always ended up owing me two dollars.

The second spring after we were married, Lovina's father died of a heart attack. During the last six months in service, I started working on my days off for Ray Norris, a mink farmer. After the two years of service were completed, we moved north of Wooster to the mink farm, where we lived in the old farmhouse. My job involved mink breeding, feeding, skinning, and building responsibilities. In February, 1962, our first daughter, Mary Elizabeth, was born.

In the spring of 1962, an eighty acre farm came up for sale close to my parents' place west of Holmesville. With help from my wife's family, we bought this property and moved there later that year. The following spring, our second son, Mark, was born. I had worked, off and on, for my brother-in-law Homer Coblentz in a painting business for the three years prior to my alternative military service. We painted mostly silos, barns, houses, and other farm buildings. We did both spray and brush painting, but the majority of the jobs were spraying. After we moved to our new farm, I bought Homer's painting equipment and, along with farming, started paint contracting work. Initially, we painted mostly houses and barns. In the fall of 1962, we got several contracts to sandblast and paint bridges for the county road system in Holmes County. In the spring of 1963, we bid on a state guardrail painting contract and got the contract. The job involved cleaning and painting guardrails in Geauga and Lake County. After finishing our other job obligations that spring, we bought some additional equipment and by mid-summer had moved our base to Geauga County.

It was an interesting new experience for our crew. I hired a number of new workers. Eighteen-year-old David Kline, now a self-educated Amish naturalist, writer, and farmer, worked for us that fall. We made new friends in a part of the state that wasn't familiar to us. Geauga County has the second largest Amish community in Ohio. In the mid-1880's, Samuel Weaver, a brother to Great-great-grandfather Benjamin Weaver, had been the first Amish settler in Geauga County.

That summer, we kept our equipment at John Miller's farm and stayed with them at their farm along State Route 168, northwest of Parkman. After completing this contract in October, we moved our equipment back to Holmes County.

An Abrupt Turn
In the Road

THE GEAUGA COUNTY JOB WAS COMPLETED THE SECOND week in October that year. I had a week's worth of farm work to catch up on after returning home. When this was completed and the weather continued mild, we agreed to paint several sets of farm buildings in our immediate neighborhood. On October 17, while setting up to paint a barn just a half mile from home, an incident occurred that led to my entering college and eventually to a career in medicine.

Our home consisted of an older house and barn. We had a large yard with a lane running along one side of the yard to the barn and surrounding fields. On that morning in October, David, our three year old son, and Mary, then one-and-a-half years old, were playing in the yard. Sometime after they had gone out, David came to the door with Mary. She had fallen, or was hit with something, resulting in a large laceration across her chin. Since I was working close to home, Lovina brought Mary to our job site. After I cleaned up, we took Mary to the emergency room at Joel Pomerene Hospital in Millersburg. There Dr. Charles Hart took care of her injuries and sutured her laceration.

After leaving the hospital, we headed back to the paint job. When we got close to home we noticed smoke, and a little later, heard a fire truck. Both were in the direction of our job site. My employee that day was a young Amish boy who today is an Amish deacon. He had filled the compressor engine with gasoline and spilled a small amount. When he pressed the starter, a spark ignited the gas fumes and set the truck and equipment on fire. It was out of control from the start. He nearly killed himself trying to keep the fire from spreading to the barn and other outbuildings. This allowed enough time for the fire department to arrive, get the fire under control, and save the buildings.

The truck that burned contained our big compressor, paint tanks, hose, paint, and other equipment. The next day, I contacted Paul Hummel, our insurance agent, regarding the losses. Paul was also pastor of Berlin Mennonite Church. The following week, I met with Paul at his home on several occasions. During these exchanges we discussed various subjects, including my work, future goals, and what I thought at the time were unrealistic dreams. Somehow over these short bits of conversation, he convinced me to come to his house the following week to take a GED (General Education Development) test. He first followed an argument that taking the test wouldn't commit me to anything. We had initially gotten on the GED subject when I told him that I once entertained thoughts about some kind of work in the health profession.

My next problem was how much to tell Lovina. Since nothing would likely come of it, my initial plans were not to tell her I was taking the test. However, the day before taking the test, I

Paul Hummel

had second thoughts about taking it behind her back. This led me to tell her about the test. When she didn't respond negatively, it was left at that.

Meanwhile, Paul had contacted Eastern Mennonite College in Harrisonburg, Virginia. He was thinking several steps ahead throughout the process. He knew before I took the test that I would be accepted as a conditional student if I did well and wanted to attend. This takes us to the night of November 2, when I went to the Hummels' house after work to take the test. Lovina's November 2, 1963, diary entry says, "Wayne took a test at Berlin." Several weeks later the ante was increased when Paul called to tell me I did well on the test. Now what was I supposed to tell Lovina? I realized the whole proposition was unfair to her. Less than a month before, I had nothing even remotely in mind of this nature. I got the test results back the day before President Kennedy was assassinated. That was a shocking event and it seemed to put our life on hold for several days. Our neighbors, Fern and Lura Bowers, called Lovina right after it was reported on the news. Lovina came to the barn to tell me. We spent the rest of the day watching the news at their house.

It wasn't until the next week that we got back to discussing the implications of the test I had taken several weeks before. When I had told her about taking the test, she had asked no questions and I had offered no explanations. I now experienced a feeling similar to when I wanted to ask Father if I could go to high school. It never got done because I felt it would upset him, and I knew what his answer would be anyway. This time, I hoped, would be different. Lovina's initial response to my, "What would you think about moving to Virginia so I can go to school?" was mostly surprise. It turned out, however, that we had a good discussion on the subject. We considered the impact on ourselves and on our families as best we could as the first issue. Next came the church question, what would be their position? The third major question was, could it be done financially? Since medicine was the only real goal I had for going to school, what if I couldn't get into medical school? A mixture of faith and self-confidence kept me pushing ahead. I didn't realize how deeply this decision affected Lovina until after she died, twenty-six years later. From November 23, 1963, until March 28, 1964, she didn't write anything in her diary.

Once the decision was made to proceed, the next chore was letting our families, friends, and the church know of our contemplations. There were few surprises for us. Only about three or four families from the church openly encouraged us. Even those that did had many reservations. The same was true in our immediate families. The reservations of so many people made it a lot harder for Lovina than for me to stick to our plans. We decided that it was a faith proposition from the start. It was clear that logic would leave us with too many gaps to fill. Most of our family and church friends felt it wasn't the right decision for a boy who was brought up Amish. Most of our other friends— other than Paul Hummel—thought it was foolish. It seemed clear that faith was our only recourse. How else could I propose to take my family—including Lovina, now pregnant with our fourth child, David, three, Mary, two, and Mark, who wouldn't be one until March, to Virginia? Most of our family, friends, and the church fellowship thought it was a wild goose chase at best. It was good we couldn't foresee the future. Many were the times, had we known everything, that we would not have had the courage to continue.

In mid-December, 1963, Eastern Mennonite College officially informed us that I would be accepted as a conditional student for the second term of the 1963–1964 school year. We made one short trip to Harrisonburg in December to see the campus and to rent an apartment from the college. Following that, we arranged to have a public sale. In early January, a few personal possessions and all of our farm equipment and supplies were sold at public sale. This all happened so fast that two people I had business accounts with showed up at the sale for their money. The farm and house were rented out before we left. My father helped look after the place until we sold it to my uncle Emanuel. The final days before moving were difficult for Lovina. She wanted very much to stick to our plans and yet she dreaded parting from our extended families and other support groups and friends. Having three small children and expecting a fourth seemed responsibility enough without opting for all the unknowns before us.

The College Years

WE MOVED TO HARRISONBURG, VIRGINIA, THE SECOND week in January. Two men from our church, Ura B. Miller and David Miller, took our household furniture and goods in a large truck. Lovina and the children went with me in our car. The next week, as a twenty-six-year-old freshman, I started my initial semester classes. We had enough finances to get through that semester. In the back of my mind was the possibility of not being able to master the academic work, but I never let myself get preoccupied with this. I did nearly all my studying at home. Some of the classes seemed silly, initially. The only one I had difficulty with was what they called "new" math. This provoked me because, if anything, basic mathematics was my strong suit.

Nevertheless, I soon got adjusted to the life of a student. The term passed quickly. Before we knew it, it was time for Lovina to return to her family in Ohio for the last four weeks of her pregnancy. On May the eleventh, my brother Lester and sister Mary

Ann took Lovina and the children back home to Ohio. They went to stay with her mother, Emma, her brother Homer, and her sister Mary at their farm near Mount Hope. I stayed in Harrisonburg to finish the semester and take final examinations. We still had our place in Ohio to fall back on if school didn't work out.

On the next to the last day of tests, one of the instructors gave me a note informing me that a daughter had been born to us the day before. Lovina was doing well and the little girl's name was Lois Ann. Lois was born at Joel Pomerene Hospital in Millersburg. Dr. Charles Hart attended the delivery. His bill was twenty-five dollars. Lovina had worked for the Harts, helping with the children and the housework before we were married. I passed all the courses and could now get into the regular curriculum for the next school year if I so desired.

On June the fifth, I returned to Ohio to be with my family and new daughter. Soon after, we moved to a small "*daudy*" house on the Homer Mullet property near Lovina's home place. I resumed my paint contracting work during this time. We decided to continue with school plans. Before returning to school that fall, I sold the paint equipment to LeRoy Coblentz, one of the employees who worked for me that summer.

Back in school that fall and winter, I sold hay to farmers in the Harrisonburg area. Because of dry weather, there was a big shortage of hay in the Shenandoah Valley. My brothers, Dan and Lester, bought the hay in Ohio and helped arrange shipping it to Virginia by truck and rail. This income and Lovina doing housecleaning work, plus twelve hundred and fifty dollars in student loans per semester, got us through the next few terms. Selling hay during winter months was also done the following year. The first winter we sold over 500 tons. During the next two summers, I hauled Virginia-grown peaches back to Holmes

County, Ohio, where there was a large market among the Amish for canning peaches. We had eight to ten outlets for peaches in Holmes County. My sister-in-law, Phyllis Weaver, and other family members and friends helped us sell the peaches. John Miller, in Geauga County, also sold peaches for us. We had stayed at his farm during the guardrail painting job two years earlier.

The first summer I bought and hauled peaches, we had a major crisis. I had gone to Spartansburg, South Carolina, to buy an early load. They were nice, tree-ripened peaches. For some reason the orchard manager talked me into having the peaches washed. When this tractor-trailer load arrived in Sugarcreek, Ohio, at my sister Fannie's place, we were in for a surprise. Most of the four hundred and some bushels of peaches were moldy. It turned out that after they were washed, they were put in the trailer before they were dry. Here they sat for another twenty-four hours before being shipped—enough time to grow a healthy mold. I was sick at heart. Visions of losing the potential profits for the whole summer floated before my eyes.

My sister Fannie thought we should sort as many as we could and we proceeded to do so. She completed the hot messy job the following morning. After the entire load was sorted, we delivered the good ones to the prearranged outlets. Nearly half the load was salvaged in this way. After some pleading with the orchard, they discounted enough off the purchase price to let me break even on the load. Few times in my life have I felt as discouraged as I did on that occasion.

Lovina canned or froze all our fruits and vegetables just as she had done at home in Ohio. Our families in Ohio canned for us too. Beef and pork we bought by the quarter or half. This was frozen and stored in the freezer. When chicken was on sale, Lovina bought it in large lots and froze it. On days I could babysit, she continued to do outside housecleaning one or two days a week. At the end of the second year we sold our farm in Ohio. That freed up several thousand dollars, enough to keep me in school. Eating out was unknown to us. I don't think our children knew what that was until they caught on after starting school.

Our introduction to the wonders of day-old bread, pastries, and dairy products came about in an interesting way. When a trip was planned to Ohio during the 1964 holidays, we watched the bulletin board for students needing a ride. One student would be enough to pay for the gas for the trip. The first time we did this, Carlene Holsopple from Davidsville, Pennsylvania, was our passenger. It was late in the day when we got to the Holsopple farm. We accepted their invitation to stay overnight. They got day-old baked goods and dairy products from stores to feed to their hogs. They had just received a shipment before we arrived. The delights of these goods were soon a favorite of the children. From this trip on, the children always wanted to go by the Holsopples'. When we could, we stopped on the way back to Virginia and loaded the trunk for the return trip. Later, Lovina found a day-old baked goods store which we patronized in Harrisonburg. A bonus on that first trip was the unexpected discovery of my immigrant ancestor Jacob Weaver's grave on the Holsopple farm. Anna Yoder, who still teaches school at Mount Hope, was a frequent passenger for the Ohio trips. In addition to sharing the fuel expenses, she entertained the children en route.

In spite of being told that I never learned proper study habits, I continued to get above average grades. Going from the eighth grade at age thirteen to college at age twenty-six created some problems. The biggest one for me was study discipline. The feeling that I wasn't doing anything worthwhile if there was no physical work involved was, I believe, subconsciously a problem for me. I continued to do all my studying at home. In spite of the sciences required for a pre-med major, I enjoyed history, the arts, and current events courses the most. I drew political cartoons for the school paper the last two years in college. The hard sciences, especially chemistry, were difficult at first. A pre-medicine major required three years of chemistry. This and physics were my most difficult courses in college. The second year, I participated in a model United Nations session at Duke University. Another extra-curricular activity I enjoyed was serving as student chair of the Spring Fine Arts Committee during the third year.

Helpful people in college were, among others, student-wise, Samuel Weaver, and faculty-wise, Dr. Daniel Suter. Sam helped me work at my rough edges without seeming to do so when I first arrived. I was pushed to get enough courses in three years and one summer term to graduate. The first semester courses during the first year were conditional courses that didn't help my major requirements. Because of this and my lack of a high school background, I was frequently faced with courses without the prerequisite information. This also put me in a position to take the MCAT (Medical College Admission Tests) before I had taken a number of the required science courses. All the way through school, including medical school, I had to take some courses in which I lacked a basic background.

Physical education courses that were required—and involvement in some of the intramural programs—kept me fit during college. Hauling and unloading hay served that purpose, too. With the help of other students, we often delivered a load of hay in the morning before classes started. Eugene Hostetter was the physical education instructor. Several summers earlier, when I painted part of the Wayne County courthouse in Wooster,

Eugene was assigned to watch my sling ropes and ladders. I was hired to paint the steeple and its connected wood and metal-work. We both worked for Fred Yoder, a painting contractor from Wooster. Eugene worked for him between school terms. The high work on the courthouse job was the only time I worked for Fred, who paid me what I thought was an unheard-of ten dollars an hour.

Most of the time during college, Lovina and I attended a Beachy Amish church in Mission Home, Virginia. This involved a forty-five mile trip across the Blue Ridge Mountains to Green County. Sanford Yoder was the pastor there. Later, on our trip to Central America, we visited the Yoders in their new Costa Rica home. On Sundays when we didn't go to Mission Home, we went to one of the Southeast Conference Mennonite churches in the Harrisonburg area. A few years later, when we returned to practice medicine, we transferred our church membership to this conference.

When I graduated from college in the summer of 1967, we felt somewhat awkward sending graduation invitations to our families. It wasn't the sort of thing Amish people did. We expected no one from our immediate family to come for the graduation services. At the time, I still felt a little out of place going to college. I wasn't exactly embarrassed among old friends and family, but the less attention we brought to what I was doing, the easier it was to relate to them. In the back of my mind, through all my years in school, was Father's pragmatic view of learning. It took a lot more than a wall full of diplomas and licenses and other credentials to impress him. The implied question in the end was going to be, "Yes, I see the papers on the wall. Now tell me, what can you *do*?"

Medical School Years

IN THE FALL OF 1966, I APPLIED TO ONE OSTEOPATHIC SCHOOL, and to two medical schools. I was interviewed at all three schools and was accepted by two of them. At the third school, I was put on the alternate list. No one has ever confirmed it to me, but my going to the University of Virginia School of Medicine, I believe, had a great deal to do with an unsolicited recommendation I got from Dr. James Cash. Dr. Cash retired from the university after a long term as Chairman of the Department of Pathology. He was also chairman of the Admissions' Committee for many years.

Over the previous two summers, I had bought several thousand bushels of peaches from his orchard. It wasn't until the end of the second summer that I discovered he was a medical doctor. I often brought several of the children along when we came for peaches. This frequently involved waiting for the pickers to fill out loads. He had a black maid that seemed like part of their family. She would entertain the children and serve drinks and snacks while Dr. Cash and I visited. During one of these chats late that summer, he inquired into my background and what plans I had for the future. It was then that he told me of his life's work and experiences, and his relatively recent retirement. He told me of travels he had made to the mountains of Afghanistan where he had done extensive hiking. He knew Walter Reed of yellow fever fame. At the time we met, he was still working as a part-time pathologist at Martha Jefferson Hospital in Charlottesville, Virginia. He asked me to send him my grade transcripts from college just before I applied to medical school. He encouraged me to apply to the University of Virginia School of Medicine. I wrote him a letter thanking him for his support and recommendation. I always regretted not having maintained a continued contact with him. Our last direct contacts with Dr. Cash were through Lovina when she went to get her summer canning peaches.

My admission acceptance letter from the University of Virginia arrived in early January 1967. The rest of that school year was a hive of activity. I had to get satisfactory grades in all my classes that semester, and for the short summer term. I need-ed to get the required credits to graduate. We made several trips to Charlottesville to look for housing and to make plans for David to start school. We didn't want to live in town because of the children. We couldn't find anything affordable out of town that was close enough to the medical school and hospital. After several trips and appointments with real estate agents, we decid-ed to look at the possibilities of building a house.

We had several sessions with bankers and savings and loan institutions. The most hopeful one laid out our financial status as somewhat grim ... but. He told us that our college debt was-n't the problem since it was government secured. Just "not having any money" was. He assured me that a good credit record from the hay and peach business which I had to finance with borrowed money, was in our favor. He told us if we could beg or borrow five thousand unattached dollars he would loan us the balance needed to build a house. Since we needed another five thousand for school expenses we actually needed to raise ten thousand dollars. This seemed pretty impossible for us that summer. After a lot of thought we made a list of people who we felt might be in a position to help us raise the money. For this to work, the people involved would have to loan us money without security. Our promise to pay would have to suffice.

I contacted my wife's brother, Paul, and related the proposition to him. He was helpful and got several other church brothers committed to helping. They were Harry Weaver from Fryburg, Ohio, and Roy Mast from Berlin, Ohio. Irvin Hochstetler, an Amish businessman from Mount Hope, was also involved. We next got a promise of two thousand dollars from Andy and Joe Hershberger in South Carolina. The balance was provided by Emanuel E. Mullet. This was my father's cousin who had taken my father along to Lexington, Kentucky to buy horses. With this money in hand, we went back to the bank and found them as good as their word.

The next step was the purchase of a five-acre lot just off Hydraulic Road northwest of Charlottesville. We moved into a mobile home at the edge of Charlottesville on the first of August. The basement for our home was dug out the week before I started medical school classes. With the help of Mission Home church members, many of whom were builders, the house was completed in time to allow us to move in on Thanksgiving Day. The Mission Home church was our family's place of worship during my four years in medical school. It was closer to us now than when we attended there from

Harrisonburg. Monday, September 4, 1967, was my first day of medical school.

We moved into our new home less than a hundred days after we bought the lot. This worked out well, but even so, we were living from hand to mouth all through medical school. All our friends' grocery bills were over twenty-five dollars a week; ours was still less than fifteen. Even so, thanks to Lovina, we ate well and none of our family ever went hungry. I didn't witness children going to bed hungry until later, when I spent time in voluntary service in Honduras and Liberia. But there was another price to pay. Medical school work was much more demanding and difficult than college. I got behind in one of my classes. A trip to the Dean got me a scolding for thinking I could do medical school work with less than "one hundred percent of my time and effort." Nevertheless he heard my plea and allowed me to drop the course. I had to make this up by taking an intense summer course at Columbia University in New York City.

The summer I had to take the make-up course at Columbia we were especially hard up. When I found out the blood bank at the university paid twenty dollars for a unit of donated blood, I donated as frequently as I could. Lovina and the children stayed in Virginia while I bachelored in a student housing dorm in upper Manhattan. Halfway through the six weeks, Lovina and the children came to visit. We arranged to meet at a rest stop on the New Jersey side of the George Washington bridge. I went there by bus. Fifteen minutes after I arrived, they drove in. Lovina didn't want to drive in New York City.

The first two years of medical school were difficult, especially the first one. School demanded all my time and effort. In the past, I was seldom accused of lacking self-confidence. In my experience, serious focused effort usually sufficed. I now began to seriously question my ability to master the volumes of information demanded. My "I-can-jump-higher, run-faster, think-quicker" approach to life didn't work in this setting. To have to acknowledge that I was a very average student was humbling. Things like physiology, biochemistry, neurochemistry, and molecular biology didn't really begin to fit into a coherent scheme until the end of the second and first part of the third year. Thankfully, the big picture clarified itself during the last two years of medical school. In retrospect, I think my failure to keep in contact with Dr. Cash was in part a feeling that I had let him down; I had expected to be a better than average medical student. My self-confidence was sorely tested those first two years. The latter part of the third year and the fourth year seemed like nearing the completion of a jigsaw puzzle. The closer I got to the finish, the easier and faster it went.

I remember one day at the cadaver table listening to my three partners discuss doctors' incomes. That night I told Lovina what they said. Several of the guys had physicians in their families, or as family friends, and talked of earning as much as thirty-five thousand dollars the first year of practice. Lovina and I had a good laugh. We decided I must have misunderstood. No one made that much money!

An addition to the family took place in the third year. During the second year in medical school, Lovina started to care for newborn infants needing temporary care. Abortion wasn't legal, which resulted in more single mothers going through the adoption process after birth. Our family cared for seven different newborn babies for periods of three to six months. They all came directly from the hospital nursery to us. Income from caring for these babies helped us significantly through the last three years of medical school. The sadness and loss when the babies left to go to their adoptive homes was difficult for all of us. This was especially so for those we had a full six months.

One morning I was called to the office of one of the surgical staff. I knew this doctor but had no involvement with him as a student. After asking me to sit down, he explained that the Social Services Department had given him our name. His wife had just given birth to a little girl with Down's syndrome. They had reached a decision to have her placed in a home, but more time was needed to pursue the possibilities available. Their family was in the middle of preparing for a move across the country where he had accepted the chairmanship of the surgical department in a large hospital. Did I think my wife could help? A telephone call arranged for a meeting with Lovina that evening.

In the end, their little girl, Judy, spent the next four-and-a-half years as part of our family. When I first started to practice in 1973, Judy was taken by friends in Lancaster County, Pennsylvania. When Judy was in her young teens, Lovina and I were still Mom and Dad to her. Our family learned to love and appreciate these special children in a way that I believe will positively affect each of us the rest of our lives. She was a sweet likable child and our extended family all came to love and accept her.

At the beginning of the third year, as patient contact started on a regular basis, I realized my aspirations were being fulfilled. The first part of the National Boards were taken, passed and were now history. The various clinics gave me opportunities to relate to real live patients with real problems. The last years in medical school further confirmed my earlier intentions to go into family practice.

My experiences with physicians in my childhood were all with family doctors. As a child, I had had frequent bouts with strep throat. Trips to Dr. Nevin Mayer in Apple Creek, and later to Dr. Mitchell in Fredericksburg, are well remembered. When we moved west of Holmesville, Dr. Patterson was our doctor. All of the trips I can recall, except one or two, were by buggy. Dr. Patterson took out my tonsils when I was eleven. He was a soft-spoken, kind person, whom I could relate to as a child. I recall numerous house calls that he made to our farm home. Later in life, I made a house call to his house to care for a member of his family. The birth of all ten of my parents' children were attended by our family doctor. We were all born at home except my youngest brother.

My experience as an operating room orderly at Wooster Community Hospital had exposed me to a wider range of physician specialties. Neither that nor the years in medical school changed my intent to become a family doctor. During the fourth year, I applied for a slot in one of the new residency training programs being offered in family practice. Being in family practice was where I saw the kind of doctor-patient relationship with which I felt most comfortable.

A Summer Break

Lovina and I had planned to work as volunteers in an orphanage in Honduras the second summer after I started medical school. This was made possible by a student loan. It was easier to get health profession student loans for activities the school encouraged. Because of the physiology course I had to take at Columbia University, we spent three weeks in Central America instead of the six we had planned. We met many friends from former years. Some, like the Sanford Yoders, had moved there; others were in voluntary service. We visited British Honduras, Honduras, Guatemala, El Salvador, Nicaragua, and Costa Rica. The rest of the time we spent at an orphanage west of San Pedro Sula, Honduras.

While we were in Honduras that country got into a short war with El Salvador. It apparently started over the outcome of a soccer game. There were several bomb craters at the airport when we landed in the capital, Tegucigalpa. An American officer at the airport told us that the conflict didn't have much potential to escalate. He assured us that neither of the countries had the manpower or materials needed for war. In our travels, we were stopped at a number of roadblocks. At one, a young teen stuck the barrel of a World War II vintage 30-06 rifle into Lovina's side of the car. The gun's barrel was within inches of her nose. His obvious unfamiliarity with guns was scary. We were in a line of cars, about ten or twelve from the front, at the time. It took us several minutes to realize that we might have a solution to our problem.

James Webb, a retired foreign service officer had built a home next to ours outside of Charlottesville. He had spent the previous twenty-five years in Central America as a foreign service officer at various United States embassies. Before we left, he prevailed on me to let him type a cover letter to prominent government officials in Honduras with whom he was acquainted. He told me, "You never can tell, so take it just in case." The letter was written in Spanish. We had picked it up just before we left. It was in the glove compartment of the car. Lovina, with the gunman's permission, got it out. The next problem was soon apparent. He couldn't read. The letter, however, seemed to give him an air of importance. He promptly proceeded to go to the officer-in-charge at the head of the line. After looking at the letter, the soldier came back, waved us out of the line and sent us on our way. I still have the letter.

We had an interesting visit to the new Amish settlement at Guanimaca, Honduras. The building of a school, an orphanage, and family homes and outbuildings were in various stages of planning and construction. It seemed to be an industrious new settlement at the time. Because of the shortened trip we didn't get as involved in voluntary service as we had planned.

We spent a week at the orphanage outside San Pedro Sula,

where we were exposed to third world conditions and problems for the first time. O.B. Towery, a fellow medical student, had spent the whole summer term there. O.B., along with Lovina and I and several others, took a hundred pounds of wheat into a back country town where the Honduran government was holding between seventy-five and one hundred El Salvadorians captive. Word had gotten to us that they were confined in a town building without food. We took several bags of whole wheat grain to the town. On the way, we got stuck in the middle of a mountain stream and drowned the engine. With input from several of us, we got the engine restarted. After arriving in the town, we prepared the wheat by boiling and adding salt to it. I believe we added powdered milk to it before it was eaten. I remember finding it not tasting too bad. The prisoners were held in an old church building. We left enough ingredients for them to prepare several more meals. Our efforts were appreciated by the Salvadorians.

O.B. had some excitement several days before we arrived at the orphanage. He was caught in a crossfire while walking to his house one evening. He avoided injury by throwing himself into a low area in the roadside ditch.

All too soon, we had to return to the demands of school. O.B. Towery was one of the four students at my cadaver table. We formed a friendship that lasted through the four years of medical school. He went into a psychiatric residency after graduating.

Residency

WE VISITED FAMILY PRACTICE RESIDENCY PROGRAMS AT Akron City Hospital in Akron, Ohio, at the Geisinger Clinic in Williamsport, Pennsylvania, and at Lancaster General Hospital in Lancaster, Pennsylvania. There is a large Amish community in Lancaster County. We chose the Lancaster program because Dr. Nick Zervonas presented himself and the program in a very positive way. We felt fortunate to be accepted there. The program had a good balance of internal adult medicine, pediatrics, surgery, and obstetrics. It was a large hospital with over five hundred beds.

Family Practice was the only residency training program. This allowed for more intense involvement in some of the specialties. We didn't have to share patient care with other, specialized, residency programs. Our program addressed the increasing problem with drug and alcohol abuse. A neuro-chemical basis for the addictive diseases was taught in their program before it was generally accepted. This early background was the basis for my involvement in substance abuse treatment and prevention in later years.

In Lancaster, we lived east of the city, in Smoketown. Many of the neighboring farms were owned and farmed by Amish families. We noticed that these Amish used mules for their heavy farm work. Other differences from the Amish community we came from were their buggies and the women's head coverings.

With our common language, our family soon had friendships established in the Amish community. We went to the Weavertown Beachy Amish church. I still wore the beard I had grown since we were married. Living in the Smoketown area put us in close proximity to several private church schools. We enrolled our children in Locust Grove Mennonite School.

The residency years were extremely demanding on our time. Every other week during the first year, we were at the hospital from Friday morning until Monday night. When we were on duty the residents did nearly all the admission work-ups for the services required. The constant exposure and demands from the patients and teaching staff taught me an organized approach to health care and problem solving. I had some of my most humbling, as well as my most rewarding experiences since the start of college during these years.

The second year of the residency program, I spent a good portion of my time at a family practice training office in Quarryville, in southern Lancaster County. The office was operated much like a private practice. We had our own nursing and secretarial staff. Our patient work was monitored by one of the experienced physicians on the family medicine staff. They were available for consultation any time, day or night. Many of my patients in Quarryville were Amish.

I also rotated through the different medical and surgical services at the hospital during the second year. These included general surgery, obstetrics, orthopedics, pediatrics, cardiology, radiology, and several other sub-specialties. By the end of the second year, I was thirty-six years old. My age and the need to start paying off debts led us to the decision to start a medical practice after the second year. A third year of residency would have to wait. Once this decision was reached, we had to decide where to locate and start our practice.

Serious consideration was given to three areas. Lancaster, Pennsylvania, our home area in Holmes County, Ohio, and the Shenandoah Valley in Virginia. The latter was close to where I went to college at Harrisonburg. We were contacted by the local Ruritan clubs in Weyers Cave and Grottoes, Virginia, in the winter of 1972. Following the initial contacts, we visited the area several times in the winter and spring of 1973. After considering and looking at several of the other options, we chose to go to Weyers Cave. We were uncertain of our acceptance in Holmes County. In retrospect, I suspect that we shouldn't have been. The Family Practice Residency was a great help in the planning stages—for both the building and staff development—at Weyers Cave.

Two local physicians, Dr. John Kidwell, who formerly practiced in Weyers Cave, and Dr. Tanner, a family doctor in Grottoes, encouraged us to come to Weyers Cave. During the initial visits, Carroll Cosby, the committee chairman for the local Ruritan clubs, got us in contact with Cletus Houff and his father H.L. Houff. The Houffs owned and operated a large trucking company in Weyers Cave. We had several meetings with Mr. Cosby's committee to feel out the community's expectations. They in turn had a lot of questions about what we expected. Once we were committed to going to Weyers Cave, Cletus Houff guaranteed the loans needed to build the medical

H. Lester Houff ("HL")

facility and pharmacy. The Houff family also provided advice and oversight during the land purchase and building process. This took place at a time when the bottom line on our financial statement was significantly below zero.

We lived in a small house trailer on one of the Houff properties from June to August of that year. Ground was broken for the office buildings in July 1973. H.L. Houff served as our construction superintendent. I worked as an emergency room physician in Clifton Forge, Virginia, during the construction period. The office building was completed in late 1973. After a well-attended open house, we opened our practice in early 1974. A sad event took place that first spring. Carroll Cosby, initially the most prominent figure in our early recruitment for Weyers Cave, became ill and passed away.

We rented an eighty-acre farm on the North River branch of the Shenandoah River and moved there in August. The farm was six miles from the office. The children attended school in the Rockingham County public school system. We attended church at Bank Mennonite Church where we later transferred our membership. We had friends there from our previous four years of college in Harrisonburg.

Farm Home and Children

THE WEYERS CAVE COMMUNITY WELCOMED AND SUPPORTED us from the beginning. It was a good community in which to raise a family. One of the first jobs after we moved onto the farm was getting our wheat crop planted. Once the plowing was done, Lovina did most of the seed-bed preparation. We got the wheat sowed with the help of Calvin Baker, our next-farm neighbor. Following that, there were fences to repair for the Black Angus, Hereford, and Charolais beef cattle herd we bought the first fall. That first year, we rented the farm equipment. After the end of our one year lease-purchase contract, we purchased the farm. This time, H.L. Houff helped to finance the purchase. The following winter, we bought a tractor and enough equipment for our immediate needs. We still have the tractor and some of the original equipment.

The day we opened our office, I was $375,000 in debt. In order to make the farm more affordable, we sold thirty acres to our neighbor, Calvin Baker. The Bakers were helpful neighbors, in all respects, during our years on the farm. They have now retired from their dairy farm and have sold most of their land. The land had been in the Baker family since it was bought from the English Crown in the eighteenth century.

In 1974, most of the small outbuildings on our farm were torn down. In 1975, we tore down the south wing of the house. It was an addition to the original house, built during the Civil War era. We replaced this with a larger addition and remodeled the original structure. Our farm pond was also built that summer. We soon realized and appreciated the historical significance of the area. George Washington visited friends in Port Republic, just two miles downriver from us. Several miles farther downriver, Washington forded the river on horseback to visit other friends on a large plantation. Thomas Jefferson was also a visitor at this home. The Battles of Port Republic and Cross Keys, two Civil War battles, were fought within four miles of our farm. About eight miles south, near New Hope, another battle took place. Many local farmers have Civil War artifacts that were found on their farms.

Our home and farm buildings were located on a flat elevation approximately one quarter-of-a-mile back from the west bank of the North River branch of the Shenandoah. Looking east across the river at a distance of three miles are the foothills of the Blue Ridge Mountains. This range, from Front Royal southwest to Waynesboro, forms Shenandoah National Park. From our house, we could see short portions of the Skyline Drive, the road that weaves along the higher ridges of the park. In this area, the Shenandoah Valley is approximately twenty miles wide with the Allegheny Mountains forming its western border.

In the summer of 1977, the children and I embarked on a tennis court project. We borrowed Calvin Baker's portable concrete mixer. It attached to the three-point hitch on the back of our farm tractor. We used the tractor to grade the surface and to

prepare the base with limestone. Over the next month, we spent our spare time shoveling sand, gravel, and cement. By the time school started, we had completed a nice combination basketball and tennis court.

This was home for our children from their middle elementary years to adulthood. They learned to fish in the pond and river. The fields and woods provided their first hunting experiences for rabbits, quail, and ducks. After the boys were in their early teen years and I had an associate, we started a fall ritual at H.L. Houff's mountain cabin. We took a week off from work and school during the deer hunting season. Most years, we had one or two of my brothers and their boys as guests. Several of the boys' friends from school and the community were usually part of the group as well. In the evenings, the non-hunting family members would join us for food, games, and the stories of that day's—and previous years'—hunts. I don't hunt anymore, but I miss those evenings at the cabin each fall.

Our home reflected in many ways our backgrounds. We had a large produce and vegetable garden and a smaller garden that included flowers. A rose garden and other smaller flower beds dotted the lawn. Lovina continued to can fruits and vegetables as in former years. She sewed nearly all the clothes for the girls until they were grown. In addition, she worked twenty to thirty hours a week in the office.

Bank Church, where we attended, was one of the more conservative Mennonite churches in the area. I had worn a full beard from the time of our marriage, seventeen years earlier. Although this church officially voiced no opinions against having a beard, some of the members in the congregation weren't fond of them. I first contemplated life without a beard when the "hippie" years arrived. When unkempt beards and less than desirable personal hygiene came into vogue, it made my decision to shave off my beard easier. In a real sense, this fad had its outcome in the general population. Doctors' offices began seeing things like scabies and head lice that for many years previously were rare. Even then, I contemplated on my beard for some time.

I had been told by one of the church elders in the Beachy Amish church that shaving off my beard would be a foreboding sign to him. When we went ahead with plans to change our membership to the Virginia church, I decided to shave it off. It was not a light thing for me to do. The weekend I shaved it off, Lovina didn't notice until I brought it to her attention. We were both concerned about how our family and friends from Ohio would interpret it. Other than the sense of community in relation to my background, my beard no longer had religious significance to me. Future years revealed no relationship difficulties from that decision. My father expressed the opinion that it was probably the right thing to do, since we no longer lived in an Amish or Beachy Amish community.

During the last years in Charlottesville, and in Lancaster, Pennsylvania, the children spent part of each summer in Ohio. Their time was split between their grandparents and uncles and aunts. They got acquainted with most of their seventy-plus first cousins over these summers. The setting was often similar to that of Lovina's and my own childhood. Trips to the local livestock auction in horse and buggy, and farm work with horses, being only a few examples. They experienced Amish church and wedding services. They learned to shock wheat and oats and helped to thrash. They took horses to the blacksmith to be shod, and were on hand when the new calves, foals, and pigs came on the scene. My brother Roy told me recently of one of the summers when our boys were at their house. David was helping Roy shock wheat. It was a hot, tiresome job. When David didn't take the suggestion to take a break, Roy asked him why. His answer was, "Father told me, boys who don't learn to stick with their work become hippies."

Wayne & Lovina,
Lois,
David, Mary & Mark

Family Practice

W<small>E</small> <small>NAMED</small> <small>OUR</small> <small>PRACTICE</small> <small>THE</small> W<small>EYERS</small> C<small>AVE</small> F<small>AMILY</small> Health Center. It was designed for the practice of preventive medicine, also known as well-care. When Lovina decided to work in the office, we followed up on the tentative plans we had arranged earlier. Judy would enter a school for the handicapped in Lancaster. With the approval of her father, she became part of the Crist King family. Here, she was loved and well cared for by the Kings until she entered Mission Home School, a home and school for the handicapped in Virginia. One of the conservative branches of the Mennonite church operates this home. Although I haven't seen Judy since Lovina's illness and death, I am periodically assured by friends that she continues to be well cared for.

Our first employees, in addition to Lovina, were Maryanne Kiser, a radiology technician; Gail Martin, an R.N., and Maxine Shreckhise, who worked in the front office with Lovina. The

Weyers Cave Family Health Center

first day we were open we started without any patients. By the end of the day we had seen fourteen. We kept long hours to make ourselves available to as many people as possible. We had evening hours two days a week and were open till noon on Saturday. A month after we opened, Dr. Tanner in Grottoes decreased his hours. Within several months, his office closed because of his illness. Later in the spring Dr. Tanner died.

This caused our practice to grow rapidly. It also made the decision not to practice obstetrics easy. We were too busy to tolerate the interruptions it would cause to patient-flow in the office. For most of the first three years, we kept long office hours. The facility was built for three physicians, but we needed an adequate patient load before the practice could afford a guaranteed salary for a second doctor. When it reached that point, my eighty-hour weeks would change to a more reasonable fifty or sixty.

A usual work day started at six AM with a ten-mile trip to the hospital for rounds. From there, it was eleven miles to the office. Office hours were from eight to five daily, with extended hours from six to nine on Monday and Friday, and eight to twelve on Saturday. One day a week several hours were blocked off for nursing home visits. Our practice included one nursing home wing with one hundred beds and two other homes with fewer patients. I provided my own night and weekend coverage for the practice.

The first year we charged six dollars for an office visit. House calls were twenty dollars. That changed when one of our Sears appliances went on the blink during the first year. Their minimal service charge was twenty-five dollars. We soon paid the price for starting our fees so low. Medicare red tape started allowing us only a certain percentage of what they called our usual-and-customary fee. Instead of six dollars, we were now allowed four dollars and eighty cents for an office visit. Several doctors who set up practice at the same time and charged nearly double our fees didn't get caught in this way. We now had to start charging for urinalysis and sugar tests. Tests that were included in the office charge before.

Jerry Selph was our first pharmacist. He and his wife rented the pharmacy building and operated a pharmacy and lunch counter. He was an expert in computer applications and programming. Through his encouragement, we computerized our practice in the late '70s. Jerry passed away in 1985. The pharmacy is now owned and operated by Dan Atwell. Dr. William Collins was the first to practice dentistry in our building. Bill passed away in 1995. Dr. Timothy Wade, the second dentist, has practiced at the Weyers Cave Family Health Center since the late '70s.

In the summer of 1976, Dr. Samuel Showalter joined the practice. Sam was board-certified in family practice. One of the early things he did was to get certified to perform flight physicals. Sam, like myself, had his FAA private pilot's license. We also worked with local industries to increase the occupational medicine part of our practice. Soon after, involvement with an alcohol and drug abuse treatment program added to our workload. Sam and I were directors for this program until I left the practice in 1991. Sam and his wife Jan moved from southwest Virginia where he had been in a group practice. They both grew up in the Rockingham-Harrisonburg area. She is the daughter of Dr. and Mrs. Daniel Suter. Dr. Suter was a professor of biology at Eastern Mennonite College. Sam was from the Broadway area of Rockingham County. He complemented our practice with a more patient and personable approach. Sam and Jan have two daughters.

We had our own x-ray unit and lab. Some of the lab tests

were done by the hospital and others were done by outside labs. Maryanne Kiser was our initial licensed x-ray technician. She was very capable and eventually assumed responsibility for all the front office, nursing, bookkeeping, lab and x-ray departments.

In 1980, we started recruiting a third doctor. After finishing his residency in family practice, Dr. Gordon Weirich joined our group. Gordon and his wife Barb moved to Virginia from South Bend, Indiana, where he trained. Gordon, among other things, complemented our practice by doing obstetrics. Finally, after seven years, we didn't need to refer our expectant mothers for their obstetrical care.

Not infrequently we saw four generations of the same family. A newborn infant coming into the practice could be seen by the same doctors as its parents, grandparents, and great-grandparents. In spite of the view that country doctors doing house calls were a thing of the past, we made many. During the years from 1973 to 1991, I made house calls almost every week. Some of the most satisfying encounters in my years of practice were during these visits, mostly with the elderly and frequently with terminally ill patients. I would have missed out on many touching and interesting experiences without these encounters. I trust the patients had mutual feelings.

I had a new experience on a house call during my early years in Weyers Cave. The son of a patient I hadn't seen before called to ask if I made house calls. His mother had been sick for several days. The family recognized that she was very ill and since she was elderly, they were looking for a doctor who made house calls. After getting directions, I told her son that I would meet him at his mother's house. When he opened the door, I realized what her problem was, even before stepping inside the house. One of the strongest acetone odors I have ever encountered hit me in the face. The woman was a diabetic with a keto-acidosis condition.

This brings to mind another simple but useful observation used by physicians as long ago as in the time of Christ. Because of the sugar excreted in the urine of a diabetic patient, early physicians gave the disease the name *diabetes mellitus*. The term means "honey-sweet urine." Most doctors and nurses are well aware of the possible implications of a bathroom floor that is sticky around the commode. It likely means that there is a male in the house who sprinkles when he tinkles, and if it's real sticky, he may have diabetes.

On one house call, a family member showed me an old moonshine still with some of the parts still intact. He claimed his grandaddy had made the best moonshine in the hollow. At another home, I was given a quart of the product in a mason jar. Those "in the know" had a unique way of testing the quality of a still's product. You poured a little in a platter and lit it. If it burned with a nice blue flame, you had a good quality product. One day I saw a patient complaining of severe abdominal pain who thought sure he was dying from bad moonshine. I didn't think to ask him if it passed the blue flame test. At a later date, he reckoned it was caused by something else.

Two Cosby brothers from Grottoes owned a water-powered mill on South River, south of Grottoes. They were in their late eighties and early nineties when I first met them. On several occasions when I made house calls to see one of them, they took me out to the mill and showed me how it operated. It was impressive to see shafts and wheels starting to turn in total silence. Even after the drive shafts and pulleys came up to speed there was very little noise. They kept the mill in running order for several years after they quit making flour.

My patients in the Weyers Cave community were, for the

most part, also my friends. A man from the area told me of his life as a boy during the Depression. His family lived on the edge of a meadow on top of the Blue Ridge Mountains. His parents would come off the mountain only a few times a year for groceries and supplies. One fall they came down to Crimora in their buggy. They had to wait for a train before they could cross the railroad. While the train was passing, something scared the horse, causing him to run into the train. Both of his parents were killed. The boy, eight, and his brother, I believe, twelve, continued to live on the mountain. Several years later, the government forced them off when the Shenandoah National Park was created. They survived by living off the land and by herding cattle for a lawyer from Crozet.

On house calls, I was given tours of many of the old plantation homes in that part of the valley. Most of these antebellum homes had interesting stories connected with them. Grape shot, lead bullets, and other Civil War artifacts were in nearly every home. Several home owners showed me places where valuables and people were hidden during the Valley campaigns. At another farm home, I was shown the old lane and woods where the patient's grandfather, as a little boy, took their horses to hide them from the soldiers. This occurred at the time of the Battle of Cross Keys. The grandfather, in his later years, took this man, then a little boy, to show him the lane and woods. I visited another old plantation home formerly owned by friends of George Washington. He had made several visits there prior to the American Revolution. I also made a house call to the old Madison Home in Port Republic, Virginia. A cousin of James Madison lived here. Another house call during the early years was more scary than interesting. This occurred in a hollow east of Island Ford, Virginia. I was stopped along a dirt road at night by a man with a shotgun. All he wanted to know was where I was going.

My weekends on-call often provided an interesting mixture of calls and requests. During flu or cold season, there were frequently any number of Saturday afternoon and night telephone calls. Many were for colds, sore throats, and earaches. When that was the case, I usually met the patients with acute conditions at the office on Sunday morning. Frequently during the summer months, I ended up with afternoon weekend mini-clinics for the neighborhood's lacerations and bruises. A number of children, now adults, will recall having their lacerations sutured and bruises dressed in our kitchen or study.

I recall several trauma oddities from my years of practice in Weyers Cave. One fall, I saw several identical injuries which I attributed to the extremely dry growing season that year. My neighbor, Calvin Baker, was chopping silage. While unloading, he used his hand to scrape a small amount of loose silage from the edge of the wagon into the auger. In doing so, he caught a finger in the drive chain, amputating the finger. Two days later, another neighbor did the same thing. The wagons were identical models of the same manufacturer. In an average growing year, the handful of silage that caused these accidents would very likely have been ignored.

On another occasion, similar injuries occurred on the same weekend to two nine-year old boys. The boys came from different families and lived several miles apart. It was at the time Evel Knievel was gaining notoriety for his motorcycle jumps. After watching him on Saturday afternoon TV, each boy went to his back yard and built a jumping chute consisting of one end of a long plank on several cement blocks. A straight, smooth approach led to the end of the plank on the ground. The boys claimed that their bicycle jump went well. The problem arose when the front bicycle wheel hit the ground. In each case, the rider flew over the handle bars, landing on his outstretched hands with the arms extended. The result for each boy was two broken wrists.

During my years in family practice, I was honored to serve a number of patients who were over a hundred years old. The oldest patient I cared for was 106 when she died. She was born in 1875. Her father was a Civil War veteran who had lost a leg in the war. She remembered when her father had bought their first reaper. Before that, they had cut all their grain with a scythe.

Another centenarian was our next-farm neighbor in Virginia, Kemper Jarrels. In his late 90's, Mr. Jarrels still helped care for his livestock. Each fall, when the weather was nice, we looked forward to seeing him and his son Warren husking shocked corn in the field.

At the time of this writing, we are honored to have John Y. Schlabach, a one-hundred year old Amishman, as a friend. John Y. was ordained to the ministry in 1938. I knew of him as a child, but only recently met him through my brother Roy. My wife and I periodically visit the Schlabachs; sometimes as a doctor, but mostly as friends. He lives with his daughter Fannie and his son Noah on their farm east of Millersburg, Ohio. The farm has been in the family since the early 1830's. Next to the house they now occupy is the stone house their ancestors built in 1838. Beside the stone house sits an outdoor bake-oven. During nice weather, John Y. works in his wood shop. My wife and I each have an oak stool John Y. gave to us as a gift. He made the stools after his one-hundredth birthday. He is alert and has an excellent memory of long ago events in the area. A visit with him always leaves me with inspiration and food for thought. Recently he told me, "At my age, not too many people die."

Human Interest Aspects
of Practicing Medicine

I

ONE WINTER DAY I GOT A CALL FROM THE HOSPITAL EMER-
gency room. "Dr. Weaver," the nurse informed me, "you are
on medical call today." Each day there was an assigned doctor to
care for local patients needing admission who didn't already
have a doctor. The same doctor was also responsible for out-of-
town patients unfortunate enough to need admission. On this
cold, snowy winter day, the patient was an elderly lady who was
pulled out of a pond where she had fallen through the ice. They
guessed her to be in her mid-eighties and told me that she was
severely hypothermic. They didn't know her name or where she
was from. A trucker going down Interstate 81 saw her and
radioed to the State Police who in turn notified the local rescue
squad.

The pond where she had fallen through the ice was about

one hundred yards behind a motel. She had walked onto the ice and fallen through. Fortunately the water was only hip deep. Even so, she got stuck and couldn't get out. When I got to the hospital and took over responsibility for the patient, she was already better. Warming blankets and warm water lavages were working. But who was the patient?

The police had gone to the hotel to check for a possible missing person. When they couldn't find anyone missing, they contacted the night clerk. Through him, they found out that an elderly lady had gotten lost several times during the night. She had a pet cat she had to let out several times. Each time she went out to get the cat she couldn't find her way back. Twice, the night clerk had to be called to take her back to her own room. By the time the police had figured out that this lady was our patient, her husband had become alarmed and left the motel. He had asked for his wife in the adjoining rooms and was told at one of them that the rescue squad had taken someone to the hospital. With this news, he had left in his car to find the hospital. By the time the police got to their motel room, it was empty.

Meanwhile back at the hospital, two James Madison University coeds brought an elderly man to the hospital. They had found him walking unsteadily on crutches along Main Street. When they asked if they could help, he said that he was looking for the hospital and kept asking for his wife. He accepted their offer of help and with one student on each elbow he arrived at the emergency room. The clerk figured out right away that he was our missing link. The man, however, refused to tell us his name. When they took him back to see her, he immediately identified her but refused adamantly to tell us either of their names. The students told us where they had found him and didn't think he had a car. Meanwhile, the lady's condition was improving as her temperature climbed back towards normal. She was soon responsive and constantly asking for her cat. It appeared that she was suffering from senile dementia.

We next took Mr. No-name into the doctors' lounge and tried to coax him into telling us who he was. When that failed, I told him matter-of-factly that I would have to take his billfold away from him to see who he was. He became angry, but when I didn't relent, he gave me his billfold. When I asked about any children, he made it clear that his children were not to be told where they were. The billfold provided the children's names, addresses, and telephone numbers. Our operator soon found their son at the General Electric plant where he worked in Boston. The elderly couple had two children living in Boston. They lived in Maine. The children had made it known to their parents that they couldn't go to Florida to spend the winter as usual. She had severe Alzheimer's dementia, and he was an insulin dependent diabetic with complications.

Our daughter Lois was a student at James Madison University, just next door. I was able to contact her and to have her come to the emergency room. When she came in, we had her take the man to find his car. He couldn't recall where he had parked it. They found it in one of the large James Madison University lots just off Main Street. It was next to the first hospital sign he had come to. The car was full of empty McDonalds' bags, cups, and sandwich boxes. With input from their Maine neighbors and their children, and with the arrival time at the motel, we were able to reproduce an outline of their trip. They had left their Maine home on Tuesday morning. They had driven all day Tuesday and Tuesday night. Sometime during the late afternoon of the first day, they missed a turn-off in the New York City area and ended up going west until they intersected with Interstate 81. They continued to drive until they arrived exhausted in Harrisonburg. This appeared to have been their first stop for rest. The man told us later that his wife had used the rest room when they stopped for gas and he used a urinal. The night clerk told us that the man was so unsteady on his crutches he had to be helped to their room. Later, on both occasions when the night clerk took his wife back to the room, the man was sleeping on top of the bed covers with his clothes on.

When the man and Lois got back to the hospital, he was still upset and distraught. He wanted us to discharge his wife so that they could leave. His son filled us in on the details. His father was very upset that they were told they couldn't go to Florida. The response to this was that they had left their Maine home on Tuesday morning, two days earlier, and headed for Florida. The son was speechless when I told him the call was from Harrisonburg, Virginia. We had him talk to his father, to try and calm him, but without success. His father was so aggressive in his demand to leave that the police stood by. They offered to take him to the motel, which he refused. He also refused to be admitted to the hospital. An involuntary admission to the psychiatric floor was an alternative I didn't want to consider. We would have to get a judge to agree to hear the case during the night or he would have to spend the night in jail. He was having enough difficulty already. When we reached this stand-off, we offered to take him home to our house since he had gotten along pretty well with Lois. The man's son was agreeable to this, so Lois took him home with her for the night and his wife was admitted to the hospital. As the years go by, this kind of practical response to need is considered irrational. What if something would happen? You would immediately be sued and be held accountable for any possible adverse outcome whether you were responsible or not. It is this kind of logic that prevents a common sense, caring relationship between many patients and their doctors.

Back at the hospital, the patient became loud and extremely restless during the night. In the morning, after three calls from distraught nurses, I made early rounds. When I found no reason to keep her hospitalized, I called the office and told them I would be running late and took the woman home to the house so the elderly couple could be together. Here, she was better satisfied, but still kept constantly asking for her cat. They stayed together in the same room and had a reasonably good night the next night. By previously arranged plans, we picked up their son at the airport the next day. The following day he took his parents home in their car. His father was insisting when they left that they were going to Florida. The next day I got a call from the son. He kiddingly said that he was calling from Florida where it was cold and snowing. They were back home in New England, with his father no happier than when they had left our house.

II

One day, one of our patients hurried into the reception room from the parking lot. She informed the receptionist that a car had just wrecked on the front lawn of the office. We hurried out with a stretcher and a wheelchair. Two ladies in their late fifties or early sixties were in the car. The driver couldn't walk and her friend acted drunk. We wheeled them to the office where they both denied any pain or injuries. Both had slightly bluish, ruddy complexions. The one especially seemed short of breath. They denied the use of alcohol and had no alcohol odor. During our medical assessment their mood seemed to be inappropriate as they would occasionally glance at each other and giggle. Their lungs were clear and they also denied the use of tobacco. After the initial several minutes, we recognized that they were both breathing faster, even while at rest. When oxygen was started, their color and breathing improved rapidly. Their interactions between themselves, and with us, also took a turn for the better.

By this time, the State Police were investigating the accident. While at the scene on our lawn, the officer got a report of a man walking along the Interstate acting strangely. At the same time, the driver of the car started asking about her husband. They told us that they were driving north on Interstate 81 when her husband began talking and acting very strange. By the time they got close to the Verona exit, he was becoming very disruptive. Between there and Mount Sidney, they had stopped and let him out. As you will probably have guessed by now, they were all suffering from carbon monoxide poisoning. We kept our ladies on oxygen until the man on the Interstate was identified, taken to the hospital, and carbon monoxide poisoning confirmed. They were then transported to the hospital for further care.

After piecing everything together, we concluded that the following must have happened. After she let her husband off, the driver apparently had second thoughts about his welfare. This prompted her to take the next exit off the Interstate. This brought her to the intersection and traffic light at our office. When she couldn't negotiate through the light, she landed on our front lawn. The final cause turned out to be a defective muffler.

III

The summer Mark was twelve, we took an unexpected excursion to the northeast. I was on-call to accept out-of-town patients, when a lady from the New England states was brought to the emergency room. She and her husband were touring the area in a recreational vehicle at the time. She had a small heart attack. By the third day, she was homesick and asking to go home. After repeated requests to be transferred back to her home, I got a cardiology consult. The consultant thought it would be acceptable for her to fly home, provided she had appropriate medical personnel in attendance. When they found out it would cost several thousand dollars plus the plane fare to do this, they asked me to attend them on a regular commercial flight. Her fifth hospital day was on a Friday. Since I had two weekend days off, I agreed to travel with them on a regular commercial flight on Saturday. This included the provision that her condition had to remain stable and that she pass a mini stress-test. When she passed, we accompanied her home on Saturday morning. Mark went along.

Her family met us at the airport and took us to their home. After a phone call to her personal physician, we caught a train to Boston, from where we were scheduled to return the next morning. We got off the train and got a cab to go to our hotel. In doing so, we passed Fenway Park where the Red Sox were playing the Yankees. We decided to get out and see if we could get tickets for the ball game. The patient's husband had given me three hundred dollars and had paid our fares coming and going. He paid me in one hundred dollar bills before we left their home.

I didn't think about getting smaller change until I wanted to pay the cab fare with a hundred dollar bill. What a surprise! The cab driver became irate, told me I had no class, called me a lot of names I wasn't used to being called, and threatened to have me jailed. Being Saturday, there were no banks open. The only place open anywhere close by was a liquor store. I headed in that direction with the cab driver still yelling at me at the top of his lungs. I tried to look inconspicuous as I looked for the least expensive item I could find. It turned out to be a six-pack of Pabst Blue Ribbon beer. The clerk looked at me for a moment before checking with his boss in a back room. After a quick once-over by him, I got my change and beer and was on my way. We put the beer in the nearest trash can and paid for the taxi. The way the cab driver continued to fuss, you would have thought we had robbed a bank.

From here, we walked across the street to the ballpark. We had to pay a scalper double the regular price for the tickets. We got seats in the deep center field bleachers, about ten rows back, behind the bullpen. This was the game in which Billy Martin, the Yankees' manager, got into a shoving match with Reggie Jackson. Jackson didn't hustle enough on a fly ball to the outfield to suit Martin. When Reggie returned to the dugout, they got into an argument that led to the shoving episode. Later in the game, Carl Yastrzemski hit a long home run ball our way. I saw it was going to land in the bullpen. A group of guys in front of us stood up as the ball was coming down. When it didn't reach the bleachers they sat down. They didn't see the ball bounce out, and were quite surprised to see me catch it.

IV

In the summer of 1993, while at a county fair in Ohio, an interesting incident occurred. I was sitting with one of my first cousins, Titus Schlabach, in the grandstand watching harness races. My pager went off asking me to call the hospital. I walked across the infield to the back side of the track to use my cellular car phone. Just as I got to the car, a race started. When the horses came around the turn into the backstretch, the last sulky veered out and the driver fell off. He slid along on the dirt for 30 or 40 feet and stopped just across the guardrail from where I stood. When I ran to him, he had no pulse and wasn't breathing. A deputy sheriff was on the scene right away, too. With his help we started CPR. The loose horse continued around the track another three or four times. A line of horsemen cordoned off the rescuers and the heart attack victim from the horse passing on the inside of the track. A few minutes later a rescue unit arrived. When the monitor showed ventricular fibrillation, we cardio-verted the patient. The response was immediate conversion to a normal sinus rhythm. He regained consciousness as he was loaded for transport to the hospital. His heart had stopped after suffering an acute heart attack. The rescue squad transported him to the local hospital. The last I heard, two years later he was still driving horses.

V

The first summer after I remarried, I encouraged my new bride, LaVina, to try golf. She took to it like a fish to water. During a trip to Virginia in late spring 1994, we scheduled a tee time at Canaan Valley Resort in West Virginia. Just as we were ready to tee-off, the pro shop called the starter to see if it would be all right for another twosome to play with us. We said no problem. A few minutes later, after introductions, we were off.

At the seventh green, I noticed that one of the men was leaning on the flag stick for a moment. On the next hole, he paused for several moments on his way to the cart. At the ninth hole, he both paused and leaned on the flag stick. I mentioned to LaVina after the eighth hole that I thought he was experiencing chest pain. In spite of steering the conversation, on the way to the next hole, to let him know I was a medical doctor, he didn't volunteer any complaints. After he appeared in obvious distress on the tenth green, he admitted he wasn't feeling well and readily agreed to accompany me to the club house on my cart. LaVina and his partner went for the emergency medical bag we carry in the car.

We treated him like an acute heart attack victim, with all the signs and symptoms pointing in that direction. I had basic medications and equipment in my bag. Although we didn't have a heart monitor, we had oxygen, nitroglycerin, Lidocaine, Demerol, and normal saline iv solutions. The stabilization and pain control process was interrupted by a fainting episode. About an hour later, we were on the way to the nearest hospital by local rescue squad. A paramedic was picked up en route.

At the hospital, the man was admitted to their coronary care unit overnight. When his pain didn't stabilize, he was transferred to a larger medical center the next day. Here, he had an angioplasty procedure done. Although we haven't gotten around to it yet, we still plan to visit him at his West Virginia home. Periodic telephone and mail contact with the family has continued through the intervening years. We have long since used the complimentary passes for two additional rounds of golf that the resort provided for us.

On another occasion, when my two sons, son-in-law, and I were playing golf at the Canaan Valley Resort, we were told that our tee time would be delayed. Soon after, a big limousine dropped off several people. It was the late Secretary of Commerce, Ron Brown, who had come to play golf.

Flying Experiences

IN 1978, I GOT MY PRIVATE PILOT'S LICENSE. OVER THE YEARS, my flying has been primarily recreational and usually during clear evenings in the spring and fall. The flying range was mostly confined to the Shenandoah Valley from Front Royal to Waynesboro, north and south. From east to west we covered the Valley from the Blue Ridge to the Allegheny Mountains. Over the years, I have flown to Pennsylvania several times and to Ohio on a number of occasions.

During one trip to Ohio for a wedding, we had some excitement. Our daughter Lois wanted to meet a pen pal from South Africa. The only day the pen pal was anywhere close to us was also the day we had to leave for the wedding. She would be at National Airport in Washington DC for several hours that morning. To accommodate Lois, we flew to Washington and met with her friend. After the visit, we left for Ohio. Lovina, Lois, and David were along. As we got over central West Virginia, the

cloud ceiling kept lowering. This forced us to fly so low that the
VOR radio signals (very high frequency omni-directional range
station) were lost. This forced us to fly by dead reckoning. When
it started raining, and with clouds building up, I deemed it inad-
visable to continue. Even though we were only thirty minutes
from our destination in Ohio and had an hour of fuel left, we
started looking for a place to land.

Since the Ohio River was already in view, I decided not to
abandon a readily recognized landmark. Our map showed a private grass strip north of New Martinsville, West Virginia, so we
turned north along the river. When we couldn't find the grass
landing strip, and the rain increased, I selected a field along the
river and landed. It was just on the edge of Martinsville.We
knocked on the door of the closest farmhouse; a friendly lady let
us use her telephone to call Mark. About two hours later, Mark
picked up the others so they could make the wedding the next
day. I stayed over and got fogged in the next morning. We had
landed in a field alongside a railroad track. It was late morning
before the fog lifted. After it cleared, I did my pre-flight walk-
around and was soon ready to taxi. To gain speed, I started in
the opposite direction of the takeoff pattern. I came out of the
U-turn parallel to the railroad track. As I started picking up
speed, a freight train came along and passed by with the crew
hanging out the windows in surprise. This was a field that usually had corn growing in it or cattle grazing. As I gained speed
and passed over them after liftoff, they waved and gave me several short goodbye toots on the whistle.

Some of the most pleasant times in my life were enjoyed
with the children. Unfortunately, they were also present for the
majority of my most embarrassing moments. One embarrassing
episode took place while flying to Messiah College in
Pennsylvania with Mark. This occurred during the early years of

"with the crew hanging out the windows in surprise"

my flying.

I wanted to show Mark how competent his dad was with his flying skills. We had altered our course to avoid flying over Camp David, the Presidential retreat in Maryland. This was a restricted fly zone, which meant that planes couldn't fly over it at the altitude at which we were flying. Just after passing Camp David, I contacted the Harrisburg tower. Before I could identify myself, three fighter jets flew across, in front of us, and close enough for us to see the pilots' heads clearly. At first I thought the fighters were after me! Maybe I wasn't clear about the location of the Presidential retreat. The jets had my attention long enough for the air traffic controller in the Harrisburg tower to become irritated with my delayed reply. This in turn got me a little befuddled. As the tower gave me my landing instructions, I was thinking "no problem." Mark didn't realize there was any difficulty, so after turning on our final approach, we were about halfway to touchdown when the tower, in a very loud and angry tone asked, "*Romeo 60546*, is this the first time you've flown an airplane?" The jet planes had ruffled me enough to cause me to turn down the wrong runway. By this time, the air traffic controller must have thought it was in the public's best interest to get me on the ground. They cleared me for the runway we were on. After sitdown, I turned to Mark and lamely confessed that maybe I wasn't as sharp a pilot as I thought.

Although I have had some scary and interesting happenings related to commercial flying, a highlight of my private flying was an unexpected opportunity. One fall Saturday afternoon in 1980, my Weyers Cave Family Health Center office called and asked if Lovina and I would like a ride in the Goodyear blimp. The airport manager was a friend and a patient. Smith Transfer, a large trucking firm, was celebrating its fiftieth anniversary. Because they bought their tires from Goodyear Tire & Rubber,

The Enterprise

they had the blimp at the local airport as a center of attraction for several days. Smith Transfer employees had an opportunity for blimp rides by a raffle drawing.

The last day there, the pilot, in appreciation of the airport accommodations, told the manager he could fill the gondola with people of his choice. The call to our house got us to the airport promptly. Sam and Jan Showalter were also along. The best was yet to come. After getting off the ground, the pilot asked if anyone had a pilot's license. When Sam and I replied affirmatively, we got the opportunity to pilot the Goodyear blimp. I flew it over our farm and to Port Republic and halfway through a turn to the west when Sam took over and flew for a while. The controls were very similar to that of the airplane I flew. The responses were delayed and navigational adjustments took a number of seconds before anything happened, otherwise it was similar to flying a small plane. The speed was intriguing. We felt like we could count the flies on the cows' backs in the pasture fields below. This, like a hole-in-one I once experienced in golf, was not a goal in my life. Nevertheless, the rare opportunity and good fortune were cherished and greatly appreciated. The Goodyear blimp was *The Enterprise.* I always thought Patrick Henry was a fiery orator in Williamsburg during the early days of the American Revolution. We were surprised to have the Captain of *The Enterprise* sign our flight logs, "Capt. Patrick Henry."

I have had various unusual experiences with commercial airlines. The first one was in 1969 in Honduras with Lovina when we flew through a terrifying thunderstorm in a DC-3. When we finally got through it and were about to land, a cow appeared in the middle of the grass landing strip. We had to abort the landing and make a fly-around until a man came out and chased the cow off. Another was an instance in western

Africa, in 1991, before we landed in Monrovia, Liberia. To avoid rebel bullets, we flew low over the Atlantic Ocean waters the last fifteen minutes into Monrovia. There will be more about this later.

Coming home from Alaska in 1981, Lovina and I, along with our friends Annis and Glen Rohrer, were about thirty-five minutes out of Seattle when we noticed a sudden change in RPM. A slight change in the vibration hum that all airplanes have was followed seconds later with a course correction. About a minute later we were told that one engine had to be shut down because of dropping oil pressure. Emergency landing procedures were instituted and we spent the next forty-five minutes with our heads on pillows, on our laps, making a controlled descent over the Cascade Mountains. We landed in Boise, Idaho, clapping our hands and applauding, with fire trucks racing down the adjacent runway.

My most stressful flight experience occurred in September 1985. Our medical group served as part of the disaster plan for the Shenandoah Valley Airport. The airport is only two miles from our office. On that September morning, we were notified by the terminal manager for Piedmont Airlines that radio contact had been lost with an incoming plane from Baltimore. At first the plane was classified as *late*. A second call officially upgraded the plane's status to *possibly missing*. By the time I arrived at the airport after lunch, the plane was officially classed as missing. The state police captain in charge of the search-and-rescue operation had called a meeting. Present were representatives from Henson Airlines, the Grottoes' rescue squad, the Civil Air Patrol, the airport manager, and our office. The plane was a commuter aircraft with a twenty passenger capacity. A heavy fog that morning hadn't dissipated until nearly noon.

A copy of the plane's last radio transmission was forwarded

to the airline from the Leesburg Air Control Center. These transmissions were reviewed in an attempt to identify the plane's last location. While the meeting was in progress, two large Marine Corps *Sea Knight* helicopters landed at the airport. They were en route from Pittsburgh to North Carolina and had stopped because of fog and low cloud ceilings. I think the whole group, without a word, viewed their arrival as providential. The state police representative left the meeting to make contact with the Marine Corps contingent. Less than an hour later, they received approval from their camp commander to join in the search. The helicopters were large. Each had its Marine crew supplemented with rescue squad and Civil Air Patrol members.

I spent the rest of the afternoon in one of the helicopters flying search patterns, initially over Massanutten Mountain and later over Shenandoah National Park. Four people sat on benches along each side, looking out the windows for signs of the missing aircraft. We could also see out the back of the helicopter, over the top of a vehicle drive-on ramp. A grid-like pattern was flown to cover the wooded mountain sides. It was an interesting and new experience for me. Late in the day, one of the Civil Air Patrol planes found a suspicious area where treetops appeared to be damaged. The Patrol couldn't get close enough with their plane, because of the rough terrain, to confirm their suspicions. The other helicopter went to the site and was able to suspend low enough to identify ground damage. They got a radio fix before returning to the airport to refuel.

Only our craft had a cable winch for rescue operations. After a short discussion among the groups represented, a volunteer and I were selected to be dropped to the crash site. A heavy, leather belt-like sling that went around the waist was provided and adjusted to fit. It had a strap that ran between the legs, connecting the front to the back. A heavy metal ring in front had the winch cable hooked to it. About thirty minutes later, just after dark, we arrived at the crash site. The rotor wash re-ignited several small fires under the foliage as we hovered over the site. The need for rotor blade clearance required a drop of over one-hundred-and-fifty feet. A radio was strapped to one of my arms and a battery powered light to the other. A dry run which took place at the airport had prepared me for what was to come next.

Several minutes later I was through the side door and on the way down to the crash site. Flood lights from the helicopter lit up the mountain side. About halfway down, my sling started swinging back and forth from the rotor wash, making it difficult to get a footing when I landed. After unhooking, I worked my way uphill to the crash site. The fuselage was under heavy brush and tree cover, not visible from above. Approaching the crash site, saplings and trees up to eight inches in diameter had been cut in a swath-like path until the wings had disintegrated. The fuselage had continued on, under the trees, for approximately fifty yards. The ground around it was charred black. There were several small flickers of flame around the edges. Only the two bodies that were thrown clear of the wreckage were identifiable. The others were all charred beyond recognition. In all, there were fourteen bodies—two crew members and twelve passengers.

Earlier years of work on scaffolding, and with ladders and slings, had prepared me for this experience. I anticipated the experience more than I feared it. Although the crash site findings were not pleasant and gave me some butterflies, the trip down to the crash site and back up was actually enjoyable. After the findings were radioed to the crew, Earl Simmons of the Grottoes Rescue Squad was also dropped to the site. After we finished the crash site evaluation, we requested pick-up and were soon back at the airport.

More recently, in January, 1996, on a flight to Florida, the pilot asked if there was a doctor on-board. They wanted a passenger who was having breathing problems examined. On this occasion, it wasn't anything serious.

Travel Experiences

IN THE SUMMER OF 1972, BETWEEN THE FIRST AND SECOND years of my residency, our family took an extended four-week trip through all the western states. We drove over ten thousand miles. In the northern swing of the trip we saw the Badlands, Yellowstone and Glacier National Parks, and the Canadian Rockies. After turning south, we visited Vancouver, Vancouver Island and Victoria, Seattle, San Francisco and Los Angeles. Disneyland was fun until we lost Mark for over an hour. The Redwood Forest and the Grand Canyon were also highlights on the swing south. We traveled in a new Toyota pickup. About half the nights were spent in campgrounds and the rest in motels. Lovina had purchased a small, new, bright orange suitcase in which to keep her and the girls' head coverings ("cappa"). At Flat Head Lake in Idaho, we came to our motel late in the afternoon. Because it was so warm, everyone hurried to our room to cool off. A little later, we discovered someone had taken a liking to Lovina's little suitcase. The ladies didn't have any coverings the rest of the trip. Someone else had a surprise.

From 1974 until Lovina became ill in 1986, we went to Florida for two weeks each March. Most of the time the children went along. We frequently stayed at the H.L. Houff residence. H.L. liked to fish at least two or three days a week when the weather was nice. He adhered to this until he was ninety years old. Most of the time we had good catches of a variety of good eating fish. Stan Moore from Ontario, Canada, was his regular fishing partner and operated the boat. We usually played golf and went to spring training baseball games several times a week. Those who enjoyed it went to the beach in the afternoon and evenings.

For the Cleveland Indian fans who flock to Winter Haven now that they train there, we have a hot tip. Prior to the Indians, the Boston Red Sox trained there. We often saw several games a year at Winter Haven during those years. The first base stands sit on a level with the field. A little ways back from the stands, a chain link fence separates the parking lot from the diamond and stands. Behind the stands is a grassy slope that falls rapidly, about twenty feet, to the parking lot level. Lovina and I got seats on the top row of the stands. The stands have a roof, but are open on the sides and back. Before going any further, I need to explain some basics for the uninitiated. Right-handed batters hit nearly all of their pop fouls to the first base side. Left-handed batters do the opposite.

On the day I am describing, a majority of the batters were right-handed and the pitcher had a rising fastball. From our perch on the top row of the stands, I signaled to Mark down in the parking lot. He had only a few competitors at first. We had a signal worked out for each pitch to a right-handed batter. When it was popped towards the first base side, I pointed to where the ball was going. This way Mark could get a head start on the ball before he could see it. Lovina and I were inconspicuous in the stands full of people.

At first the boys had planned to trade-off every few innings. These plans were changed after Mark got three balls in the first inning. As more youngsters gathered around him, he got a fourth ball. Soon every time Mark moved, the whole group moved with him. We countered by having David join Mark in the parking lot. Mark now decoyed in the opposite direction and took the crowd with him. This let David free to go to where the ball was going. The boys got nine balls during the game that day. I must add that the girls were just as adept at retrieving balls as the boys. Other parks, of course, required different strategies. The recipe for this is a family with several children who are serious enough fans to not get distracted easily. By the time our children were grown, we had several orange bags full of major league baseballs. Too many favorite kids have visited our house since then, causing the bags to shrink a little, but we still have most of them. The children have gotten about a third of them autographed.

Each year, since starting my medical practice in 1973, I attended one week continuing medical education courses. In the late '70s, I attended one course that was put on by the University of Colorado in Denver. Lovina and David took me to the airport on a Sunday afternoon. When my flight was called, David told me, in jest, to get Howard Cosell's autograph when you see him. The Broncos were playing on ABC's Monday Night Football the next night. I arrived in Denver on a late night flight. There were very few people in the airport waiting areas. Hurrying down one of the corridors toward the main terminal, I overtook a man. To my astonishment, it was Howard Cosell. He was a much bigger man than I expected. I quickly dug out a slip of paper and approached him. His response to my request for an autograph for my son was, "No one gets my autograph in Denver!"

I was told the next day that Howard Cosell had had a fight with the Denver fans because of remarks he had made earlier. As a result, a sports bar was selling raffle tickets for a symbolic chance to get back at him. The tavern had set up a new television set at which the raffle winner could throw a brick the instant Howard Cosell appeared on the screen.

David and I went on a fishing expedition to northern Ontario shortly after his sixteenth birthday. It was the first trip away from home in which he helped to drive. The Toronto area was the first night's destination. After passing Buffalo, New York, we stopped for a mid-afternoon break. Over refreshments, *The Toronto Star* informed us that the Texas Rangers were playing in Toronto that night. Further scanning of the newspaper after we were back on the road, provided us with that night's lineup. The most desirable seats were along the right field line because both lineups were heavily weighed toward right-handed batters. The Toronto water front and stadium was a very pleasant setting. A few mysterious looks came our way when we asked to look at a layout of the stadium before buying our tickets. We got seats at the far end of the last open section along the right field line. During the game, there were four foul balls hit into the right field stands. We got three of them. After the third ball, part of the twenty-three thousand fans cheered us. A few booed. On the way home, we stayed in the Niagara Falls area overnight. Dinner that night was in the revolving restaurant at the top of the tower at Niagara Falls. Even though the fishing wasn't very good, making new friends, discovering new points of interest, and the ball game interlude made the trip enjoyable.

In 1981 we, along with another couple, spent three weeks in

Alaska. Camping, fishing, and back-country hiking were in our plans. We flew to Anchorage where we rented a car. We covered most of the driveable roads in the state. Allen Smith, a former boyhood neighbor from Holmes County, lived in Anchorage. The Smiths met us at the airport and took us to their home to spend the night. We ended up spending more time with them and less time hiking and camping than we initially planned. Allen and Emily were very helpful with all kinds of tips for fishing spots and other travel tips. We caught a lot of fish, mostly salmon and trout. *The Mile Post*, a travel magazine for Alaska, served us well. I try to follow my father's example when traveling. He liked to prepare himself beforehand by studying the geography and history of his travel destinations.

We were embarrassed the first morning we went fishing. It was only fifty yards from our tent to the Russian River. We each soon had a nice salmon. Shortly after, I saw two other guys half snickering at us. They threw back nearly all the salmon they caught. When my curiosity got the best of me, I walked over and asked what we were doing that tickled them. "Oh," they said, "we don't eat humpies." We later found out that the local people really don't eat pink salmon. Silvers were the ones to catch that time of year. I didn't think silvers tasted that much better than the pinks right out of the frying pan. Silver salmon do smoke a lot better though.

In the fall of 1990, Mary, Lois, and I spent two weeks in the Canadian Maritime Provinces. We drove to Washington DC, where we stayed overnight with Elmer Lapp. Elmer is the pastor of a small community church on the east side of Washington DC. Next morning, we took the Metroliner to Boston and rented a car for the trip through New Brunswick, Nova Scotia, and Prince Edward Island. It was a delightful journey. The coastline of Nova Scotia, with its lighthouses and fishing fleets, is idyllic.

Peggy's Cove, along the southeast coast below Halifax, goes back to the 16th century. Louisbourg on Cape Breton Island had over fifteen thousand people when Boston had only four hundred inhabitants. The sad story of the Arcadians' abuse by the English is documented in their villages. These were the people that provided the setting for Longfellow's poem *Evangeline*. Along the coastline, we frequently stopped for lobster and other seafood. A number of places had lobster served right at the dock.

From Nova Scotia, we took a ferry to Prince Edward Island. Large potato fields were of interest there. The native islanders claimed that a large portion of McDonald's french fries get their start in the fields of Prince Edward Island. On the northern coast, we saw them harvest seaweed. The farmers had "very sophisticated" equipment consisting of a two-wheeled rake with long tines. A draft horse in a shaft pulled the rake out through the swells as far as several hundred yards from shore. Here the horses turned around and, after dropping the tines, pulled the seaweed to shore where it was forked onto a wagon. Water reached nearly to the horses' backs when they turned around. We went to the buying station where the seaweed was weighed and sold. We were told that it is mostly used for filler in foods. One of its primary uses is in ice cream. Not far from where we saw this was the setting for *Anne of Green Gables*. During our driving, the girls read the book *Anne of Green Gables* out loud. It wasn't long before I was enjoying the story too. The girls went to see an *Anne Of Green Gables* play in Charlottetown. I do believe we had kindred spirits before we headed back to Boston and home.

In the fall of 1992, Lois, Mary, and I went to Alaska for two weeks. We stayed just outside Juneau with Rick and Susan Slatter. Rick is married to Susan Shreckhise from Weyers Cave. Her mother, Maxine, worked in our office. Rick was working for a surveyor and was away from home much of the time. Rick and Susan had both taught school in Juneau for several years. From Juneau, we took a ferry trip to Sitka where we stayed overnight at a bed-and-breakfast. Sitka was once a Russian colony. The town appears to have done a good job preserving their Russian Orthodox culture and history. The ferry made other stops along the way. Later we enjoyed trips to Haines and Skagway in a small sightseeing plane. We saw an Alaskan brown bear and quite a few bald eagles on this trip. Skagway was nearly an empty town since it was just at the end of their tourist season. We bought a lot of half-price clothes and souvenirs. Just outside of Juneau, we walked to the edge of a large glacier.

On the way to Juneau by plane, we had an overnight stay in Seattle. After an early dinner we rented a car and went to the Kingdome to see the Mariners and Blue Jays play. In the first inning, Lois caught a Ken Griffy home run ball in the right field stands. After the game, we hurried back to the hotel to watch the replay on the eleven o'clock news.

Future Plans
Are Put On Hold

IN THE LATE FALL OF 1986, LOVINA AND I WERE LOOKING FOR-
ward to a short vacation. We planned an overnight stay in the
Pocono Mountains on our way to New York City. Rick Soldan, a
family friend, kept an apartment in New York and had invited
us to use it. We planned visits to the Metropolitan Museums of
Art and History. A friend, knowing my interest in Mark Twain's
writings, told me of a play he thought we would like to see. It
was called *Big River*, and it was playing during our planned visit.

   We left for vacation the last week in November and stayed in
the Pennsylvania Poconos the first night. The trip to New York
was uneventful. Rick's apartment was on 52nd Street close to
Central Park. We had a nice two-day stay at the apartment. The
days were full with visiting points of interest. We ate at an Italian
restaurant the second night and following dinner we attended
the play. The next morning we had a late breakfast before leaving the city. As a point of interest we went to the rest stop on the

New Jersey side of the Hudson River where Lovina and the children had met me the summer I spent six weeks at Columbia
University, years earlier.

On the way home, we had a relaxed enjoyable trip driving
down Interstate 81. As we were passing Hagerstown, Maryland,
Lovina reached across and brought my right hand to a small
nodule on the left side of her neck. She asked me if I thought it
was anything to be concerned about. It was a nodule one-half
centimeter in size. I told her it was the type of thing I see in the
office nearly weekly and most clear up on their own without
treatment, but it needed to be watched. Since she had a regular-
ly scheduled appointment with her doctor in ten days, we would
just wait until then to have it examined. Several days later, I saw
her doctor during hospital rounds and mentioned the nodule.

We approached the appointment time without apprehension since the lesion was felt to have a low possibility of malig-
nancy. At the time of her appointment, her physician got a surgical opinion. Together, they decided to take a biopsy of the
node. It would be a simple out-patient procedure since it was so
accessible. The next day, the doctor called to tell me that the pre-
liminary report had raised some concern. The formal report the
next day revealed the presence of a cell type of cancer that has a
poor prognosis. My previous encounters with malignancies led
me to realize what we were up against. Further review of the
slides by cancer specialists over the next two weeks confirmed
the diagnosis and prognosis. The average life expectancy for an
individual with this cell type of cancer was less than six months.

The literature showed that a small group of these patients
responded positively to a triple chemotherapy regimen. We subsequently consulted with the Oncology Department at the
University of Virginia. They confirmed our research and
emphasized that responses to chemotherapy would, at best, be

temporary. They left the decision to treat or not to treat with us. The ride home was emotionally traumatic for both of us. We first told the children, my colleagues, and the office employees of the diagnosis. The initial period of shock was complicated by the need to reach some decision for further consultations. Our family friends and church family were helpful in supporting us during this emotional, spiritual, and physical crisis.

With the children home for the Christmas holidays, Lovina expressed the wish to proceed with chemotherapy. She was aware of the poor prognosis she faced. The day after Christmas she started chemotherapy. Because of the expected side effects, she would take a series of five-day courses as an in-patient at Rockingham Memorial Hospital in Harrisonburg. I was learning that no matter how many families with similar illnesses I had tried to comfort, guide, and help through the years, things were now different. The experience of her illness and dying gave me a new appreciation of family, church, and community dynamics. I have come to believe that humans, in order to be healthy, have basic needs that are best—maybe only—met in a combination of family, church, and community settings. The side effects of the chemotherapy were primarily confined to the five days of each treatment course. Of the long term side effects, the one that affected her the most, was the onset of gradual hair loss. As this progressed, we vacillated from denial, to anger, to crying on each others' shoulders. At other times, laughter served the purpose best. When the time for fitting a wig arrived, Lovina accepted it better than Lois and I did. We experienced some honest chuckles while trying the various styles.

During the time of these treatments, Lovina expressed a wish to have an anointing service at home. She asked for the service as described in the Book of James 5:15–16 *"And the prayer of faith shall save the sick, and the Lord shall raise him up; and if he has committed sins, they shall be forgiven him. Confess your faults one to another, and pray one for another, that ye may be healed."* In the presence of our ministers and several close friends and family members, anointing was administered at our home. Everyone present experienced a sense of love and joy in the Lord after the service. Lovina expressed that she would not be willing to trade the experience even for a promise of physical healing. She voiced this with a resolve and conviction that carried through the two years she remained with us.

When the five courses of therapy were completed, she was feeling better than any of us had anticipated. She had lost weight and was weak but had an increasingly good appetite. When the question of going to Florida came up, she wanted to go. We flew to Florida for two weeks and had a good period of unpressured time to reflect on our married life, our children, and our faith. We talked about how in the past we had seen crisis situations increase a family's faith. She voiced her hope that it would be so in our family. In the following six months, she returned to what, from outer appearances, was her former health. Her nearly black hair grew back with only a few more streaks of gray. Tests and scans showed continued remission of her tumor growth. At times, I wished that I didn't know the prognostic details of her illness. It would have been easier to stay longer in the comfort zone of denial. In spite of her seemingly excellent health over the next year, I periodically reminded the children what was— short of a miracle—around the corner for their mother.

Some of our worst times centered around the well-meaning people who would send us testimonials of sure cures. These included trips to Greece, Mexico and various other states. These "doctors" advocated various forms of diets, vitamins, herbs, and other potions and notions. The more sure the cure, the more ignorant the writer appeared to be in terms of any real understanding of disease processes. From some of these letters, it appeared the writer was sure that there was a cure for everything under the sun. It seemed these messages were saying that there was some sort of potion for every illness that ever existed. It appeared as if they believed that if there was some way to match the right person to the right potion, then everyone would live forever. The strange thing was, nearly all of these well-intended letters came from Christians who, if asked, would claim to be living today only for the promise of a future, and far better, home. It was clear to us that the sea-water snake-oil industry was alive and well.

Coming to a place in life where spiritual tranquillity reigns in the face of death is, I believe, a gift from God. This gift, more than anything, kept Lovina from being troubled too much by these well-meaning but poorly advised folks. She was, on one occasion, convinced by a well-meaning friend to try a diet cure. This lasted only a few days until she thought she didn't feel as good and was spiritually troubled. After a week, she was feeling worse and quit it. We felt the year of remission was the best year of Lovina's life. She seemed more focused, more resolved, and less reserved. She was quicker to speak out and contribute her thoughts.

Earlier, she had expressed her disappointment at not being able to experience the joys of being a grandmother. When Mark and Carol announced that they were expecting a child, she cried with joy. Andrew, our first grandchild, was born almost exactly one year after Lovina's diagnosis. She was in near complete remission at the time. Andrew was a great joy to her over the following year.

The remission continued throughout the summer of 1988. We rented a motor home and spent a week on the shores of Lake Erie. My brother Eli and his family spent part of the week at the lake with us. On the way back to Virginia, we spent some time in Holmes County. We parked the motor home in my brother "Buckwheat's" (Monroe) lot. He provided a vehicle for us to get around in and to see and visit other relatives. Lovina and I had been close to Buckwheat and Phyllis in earlier years. These ties were renewed after the accidental electrocution of their son Doyle in May 1977.

As fall approached, the first recurrence occurred. The first signs were those involving the kidneys. These and other problems were slowly progressing when we got together for the Christmas holidays. During this time, Lovina expressed a wish to live back in Holmes County for a time before she died. She wanted to be closer to her family and friends of former years. She told me that she always felt a little cheated by the way we had left Ohio for Virginia on such short notice in early 1964.

Living expenses, as well as the expenses of her illness and mortgage payments, necessitated my continuing work. As soon as it could be arranged, we would proceed with plans to move to Ohio. When I got to the office the Monday after Christmas, Dr. Showalter had laid the *Mennonite Medical Messenger* on my desk. It was open to an article he wanted me to read. On the opposite page was a half-page ad. A doctor was needed for the emergency room at Joel Pomerene Memorial Hospital in Millersburg, Ohio. Dr. Larry Eby, Medical Director for the hospital, had run the ad. This was the first time in 14 years of practice together that Dr. Showalter had put this magazine on my desk. I called Dr. Eby the same day. He assured me that the position was available and immediately sent me an application. He told me to expect about three to four months to get my application processed and for my Ohio medical license to be issued.

With this information, I went to Dr. Showalter and Dr. Weirich to see what options were available. Sam and Gordon told me to go ahead with my Ohio plans. We would arrange the details later with the help of other counsel. It turned out that I was given a more than fair agreement for a temporary leave of absence with pay. I didn't get my license application until mid-January. The medical board advised me that it would take 12 to 14 weeks to process and issue my license. It was the first of February before I got all the information in proper form to complete the application. Lovina thought she felt well enough for a one week trip to Florida. I had previously scheduled a week of continued medical education in Lancaster which would come up right after the Florida trip. As a rule, she had accompanied me on the yearly medical education trips I had taken in the past. From Lancaster, we planned to move back to Ohio where I was expecting my medical license around the first of May. The emergency room work would start as soon as the license was issued.

We bought a new van that we could fix up with a bed in the back. We used it for the trip to Florida. After returning home, I went right to Lancaster. Lois brought Lovina up during the middle of the week. We were able to visit several old friends from residency days in the evenings. At the end of the week, we left for Ohio. It turned out that my medical license was ready before I was. The ER work started in the first part of April. We leased a furnished apartment in Millersburg so that I could be close by. As Lovina's health failed, family and friends spent time with her while I worked. In June, Lois quit her job and came to Ohio to help care for her mother. After the first week in July we returned to Virginia. Lovina's health continued to deteriorate over the next weeks. On July 24th our second grandchild, Andrew's brother, Travis, was born. Sixteen days later, Lovina quietly passed away at home. Mary, Lois, and I were with her. We told her we loved her as she took her last breath.

The support from family, friends, and our church family,

through the two-and-a-half years of her illness, smoothed our transition after Lovina's death. Rudy and Doris Soldan were special friends through this time. After a month at home, I returned to Ohio to finish the six month term I had agreed to work. Before I went back to Virginia, the children and I spent part of a week on Pelee Island in Lake Erie. Mark and Carol brought Andrew along. Travis stayed with my brother Eli's family.

Rudy & Doris Soldan

Back in Virginia, I felt like a fish out of the water. Without Lovina, I couldn't seem to get back into focus, at home or in the office. We had agreed, during the week on Pelee Island, not to make any major long-range plans or changes until I was back in the office for a year. After eight months, I approached Sam and Gordon and asked if they would consider some kind of buy-out arrangement if another doctor became available. They agreed they would if we could find a replacement. By late fall, we had recruited a replacement for me. After that was accomplished, plans were made for me to leave the practice by January 1, 1991. It was now 18 years since we had completed the new office. Since I had never entertained the idea of not finishing out my career in Weyers Cave, I had mixed feelings. Some time off was arranged in January. After that, I planned to replace a doctor in the Aleutian Islands of Alaska for six weeks. Leaving the practice left me with some guilt feelings, a feeling like I was deserting a part of my family. This sentiment would turn out to be temporary. A new opportunity unbeknownst to me was about to present itself.

My plans for Alaska were changed when the Mennonite Board of Missions called Dr. Weirich in the first part of December about an urgent need for a short-term doctor in Liberia, West Africa. Voluntary medical work always had been a part of Lovina and my plans. We were financially just reaching a point where this type of work was realistic when she became ill. The Liberian need and opportunity provided me with a new sense of purpose.

Liberia

Soon after Dr. Weirich's call, several phone calls for exchange of information started a process that led to a three-month assignment in Liberia. On December 19, 1990, a trip to New York to meet with Paul Yount and Willis Logan of Church World Services filled in a lot of the details of the assignment. It also allowed me to hear what they expected from me. They would provide for my passport and visa needs. They had tropical medicine personnel on their staff and good resource contacts for a quick study and review of medicine in the tropics. They briefed me on the social and medical needs we should expect to encounter. Videos of the fighting were shown. If plans held, they would make arrangements for me to leave as soon as possible after my travel papers arrived. A lot of other details had to be worked out at home.

Since Mary and Lois lived at home with me, the house was taken care of. We had just bought a new herd of beef cows that were to calve in December, January, and February. The girls saw no reason why they couldn't take care of the cows, so we kept them. Mark would be available much of the time also. Bringing my immunizations and public health records up-to-date as recommended took some time. Next was preparing a list of clothes, personal items, and medicines, and buying and packing them. I bought several books on West Africa and Liberia to brush up on the history of the area.

Liberia is on the west coast of Africa. It lies between Sierra Leone on the northwest and the Ivory Coast on the east. The political situation is unsettled. A war started in late 1989. By late spring and summer of 1990, the war intensified. In mid-summer, the military government was overthrown and Samuel Doe, its leader, was killed. During the summer and fall, the conflict turned into a civil war with three active fighting factions. Charles Taylor was the leader of the initial movement against Samuel Doe. A splinter group off of Taylor's forces, led by Robert Johnson was the second faction. The third group was made up of the remnants of the Doe government army. The fighting had destroyed much of the infrastructure of the country. Thousands of innocent people were killed and many more had died of starvation. Over ninety percent of the country was in control of the Taylor-led forces. An army made up of soldiers from surrounding western African nations was protecting the capital. They formed a protective shield around Monrovia to prevent the Taylor forces from taking over the city. An interim government was trying to rule with little success. This was the setting as I prepared to leave.

My departure date was set for January 11, 1991. Several trunks of medical supplies and personal items were packed. As the time for departure arrived, I kept getting lists of names of missing persons that families wanted me to try to get word to or make contact with. Often the information included where the people lived before the war and where they were last seen or heard from. After farewells, I left for New York on the morning of January 11th. The travel plans would take me to Sierra Leone through London with stops in Banjul, Gambia.

When I got to New York City, I was informed that the State Department was advising against travel to western Africa. The Marine and Navy contingents off the coast of Liberia were being transferred to the Persian Gulf. This left no way to get into Monrovia. I waited in the Church World Services office all day. When it became clear I would be stranded in Freetown, Sierra Leone, the night was spent in New York. The next morning, I arrived home disappointed. The information available indicated that it would be six to eight weeks before a means of transportation to Monrovia would be available.

With some uncertainty, arrangements were made to work as an emergency room physician in Ohio. It would involve work at four different hospitals. Since I had my Ohio medical license, I started work the following week. I temporarily moved in with my parents. On occasion, when I had worked several shifts in a row at the same hospital, I stayed at a local motel. Over the next two months, I worked in the Millersburg, Shelby, Bucyrus, Napoleon, and Mount Vernon, Ohio, emergency rooms.

In late February, Paul Yount, of Church World Services, left a message for me to call regarding the Liberia plans. On my return call, they informed me that they would have firm travel dates and times within the next several days. Subsequently, the departure date given was March 10. Plans for the final leg to Monrovia, Liberia, would be provided after I arrived in Freetown.

My emergency room work was primarily in Bucyrus and Millersburg, Ohio, at the time. My work schedule was adjusted for the rest of March, allowing for several days at home in Virginia before I left the country. The children took me to Washington DC where I left late in the evening. En route to London, I visited with a man from New Philadelphia, Ohio. He was reading an historical novel written by one of my favorite authors, James Michener. We had an interesting visit before I turned in for the night. The plane to London was only one-third full. By putting up the arm rests between the seats in the center section, I was able to stretch out and sleep for four hours. I awoke in time to brush my teeth and shave before we landed in London. There we had to transfer from Gatwick to Heathrow Airport for the next leg of the trip.

On the bus between airports, I met the most recent Liberian ambassador to the United States, Charles Brewer. He was on his way back to Monrovia as a participant in a meeting that intended to form an interim government. On the plane from Washington, Charles Brewer and another man had sat across the aisle from me.

Our plane arrived in Freetown late Monday night, March 11. I was warned to expect surprises. The first one wasn't long in coming. My luggage was lost and I had to exchange two hundred U.S. dollars just to set foot in Sierra Leone. The next surprise was that the person who was to meet me at the airport had come down with malaria the day before. By the time I got in line to file my lost luggage claim, it was between eleven o'clock and midnight. As is the case in many third-world countries, the airport atmosphere was that of pure bedlam. The replacement that was sent to pick me up had been holding a placard with the wrong name. He finally got to me by exclusion. Not all my luggage was lost. I had several carry-on pieces and a laptop computer with me. Things outside the airport were chaotic, as expected. Porters, taxi drivers, and beggars all wanted your attention.

The taxi driver matched his car well. The man's car looked worse than the Rent-a-Wreck we had rented in Anchorage, Alaska, several years before. With a prayer on my lips, I handed him my carry-on luggage. By the time the lost luggage claim was completed, my mind was telling me that my computer and video camera were already for sale on the streets of Freetown. Before we had gone a mile, I was expecting my next surprise. From the smoke and sounds belching from it, I had little hope that the car would make it to the ferry. Each mile was a godsend. My driver, like all the other drivers, practically sat on his horn as we left the airport. I had good maps of the Freetown area and knew we would have to use a ferry. After ten or fifteen minutes of driving, we came upon a line of forty or fifty cars waiting for the ferry. As we came upon the last car, the taxi driver drove off the right side of the road without slowing down. Around a fence we went with dogs, goats, and children scattering in all directions. Back on the shoulder of the road, he stopped alongside the fourth or fifth car from the front of the line. After getting out of the car and talking to someone in the tollbooth, he sat back in the car and waited.

About thirty minutes later, the line of cars started to move. A small gap appeared behind the fifth or sixth car. I covered my face as I saw what was about to happen. He laid on the horn, aimed for the gap, and floored the gas pedal. Before I got my hands away from my face, our left rear door buckled in with a crash. Instantly, there were about a dozen men yelling and beating on the car. Several were sitting on the hood so we couldn't go any farther. Horns were blaring. About the time I thought my life was in jeopardy, he glanced over and said, "Don't worry." There wasn't even a hint of concern in his voice. He got out of the car and instantly everyone was quiet. After a few seconds, they all started laughing and slapping each other on the back. He was an off-duty policeman with some clout. Before we proceeded to the ferry, the driver left the car and about ten minutes later returned with a much younger man. The first driver had to leave for police duty.

Soon after the new driver arrived, we drove on to the ferry. The cars were packed in so tight that you couldn't get the car doors open. If you wanted to leave the car, you had to crawl out of the window. I stayed with my luggage. I also learned why the first driver had bucked the line. Not all the cars got on the ferry. The unlucky ones had another three hour wait. One hour later, the taxi dropped me off at the hotel. The trip cost me forty-five U.S. dollars. I found out that only people with connections got taxi permits. Part of each fare likely ends up in the hands of the man who issues the permits.

A generator was running at the hotel. They told me at the desk to take advantage of the lights and water before the generator was turned off. Since my suitcase with my clothes was still in London, I washed my shirt, underwear, and socks before going to bed. The next morning, I found out that clothes don't dry overnight this close to the Equator. A maid pressed the shirt for me. What a surprise I had when I found a new pair of shorts stuck in one of the outside pockets of the computer bag. I found out later that Lois deserved the thanks for these. This, and a pair of booties supplied by British Air for night flights, were much appreciated over the next several days.

At breakfast, I met Charles Brewer, the former ambassador I had met earlier. His seatmate was a Mr. Hall, a building contractor from Monrovia. They had been on the same plane I was on since leaving Washington DC. At the British Air office, we were given sixty dollars for what they called "inconvenience" money. I was happy with this until I found out that the least expensive shirt and pants in Freetown cost me ninety U.S. dollars. They also informed us that our baggage wouldn't get to Monrovia until the next Monday, at the earliest. That was six days away. I prayed for patience. I needed to buy a razor, a toothbrush, shaving cream, and toothpaste. The irony was, these were all items in a night pack given to us on the plane. The sad part was, I had discarded them all before I left the plane.

Back at the hotel, I waited in the lounge and watched several—as I found out later—illegal diamond traders in action. I was told that they were Russian and were able to trade out in the open because they had paid off the police. A little later, Samuel Pieh, the Church World Service representative, met me in the lobby. He was well-versed in local customs and had a seat confirmed on the UN flight to Monrovia the next day. The United Nations had leased a twenty-passenger plane for two semi-weekly flights to Monrovia. We left the next morning from a small airport in Freetown. This avoided a return trip by taxi and ferry to the larger airport. The plane was soon headed southeast out over the Atlantic. We flew off the coast and out of sight of land. After about an hour the plane turned east and flew low, just above the water, to Payne Airport in Monrovia.

The combined west African armed forces (ECOMOG) were positioned in a perimeter around Monrovia. This line separated the rebels from the city. Except for spotty infiltrations, the rebels were kept outside the twenty mile perimeter. A noticeable change from the streets of Freetown was the absence of dogs and cats. In Monrovia, they had all been eaten the previous fall and winter, before the food ships had arrived. On the way to our quarters near the embassy, we noticed all the palm trees had been cut down. This, we were told, was also done for food at the peak of the starvation period. The tops of the palms have a pulp center that is edible.

I was hampered without my luggage for over a week. Getting my luggage taught me what the term—"to feel like a king"—means. Daily clothes washing was getting to be a real chore. I came prepared with a map of Monrovia and soon felt, if not at home, at least comfortable with the main part of the city. Each day my trip to the clinic took me through eight to ten military check points.

The people who arrived in January had done a lot of work to get the Cooper Clinic into operation. Initially, malnutrition and its associated problems took up most of the clinic's time and resources. Once the nutritional situation in the general population improved, so did the severe cases of dysentery, malaria, parasites, and all kinds of skin sores. An increase in active TB cases was clearly another offshoot of compromised nutrition. By the time I started seeing patients in the clinic, the majority of them were, as a rule, not as ill.

Trauma, including burns, fractures, lacerations, and old war injuries, was seen daily. A feeding center for the severely malnourished operated out of our basement. Initially, many young children died in spite of the center's efforts. With a decrease in the severe cases, more time and resources were now available to be directed at individuals. The weekly mortality statistics reflected this. The most severely ill now were malnourished children with cerebral malaria. Active TB cases were also increasing. Some of these were lost before the proper drugs were available.

We learned to live with the unexpected—a baby born in the street, or in the hallway of the clinic. CQI didn't appoint a committee to investigate these incidents either. Orphan children were now getting to us on a more frequent basis. The city had more than ten thousand orphans. They lived on the streets and beaches. Up until we arrived, their time was consumed in trying

to get enough to eat. Those that got sick were left to die. There was no one to look out for them. Many of these street orphans were still malnourished and were a lot sicker than the patients brought in by family or friends.

The encounters with orphans that follow were taken out of my journal: A market woman brought in a malnourished little girl. The girl knew her name and told the woman she was six. She had large skin sores, was acutely ill with malaria, and was episodically delirious. The woman went on to say that she has a small stall at the downtown market. She had seen the little girl nearly every day and thought the girl belonged to one of the other women at the market. Many of the mothers brought their little children along. They spent the day begging and hanging around the stalls. Lately, the woman noted, the girl had come to her stand more often for food. She noticed skin sores and that the girl appeared to be ill the day before. The morning she brought her in, the girl was even worse. When the woman asked her where her mother was, the little girl started crying and said that *she* was her mother. From what we could piece together, the girl had been living in the market since it was opened about two months earlier. She moved around enough so that no one realized she didn't belong to anyone. An individual child getting lost wasn't hard to imagine when you realize that there were from two hundred to five hundred active market stalls, depending on the given day and weather. The girl got her food from handouts, begging, and scraps at the day's end. She slept under the stall tables on the ground. If it rained, she slept in the open-sided storage sheds on the concrete. The woman was helpful but had several small children herself that she couldn't provide for. We kept the girl at the feeding center during the day. Her malaria, scabies, and malnourished state could best be managed this way. Each morning, the market woman dropped the child off and in the evening picked her up.

On April sixth we had a farewell party for Susan Craun. Susan was in the group of earlier arrivals who did the initial repairs at the Cooper Clinic and got it underway. Initially, the feeding center was one of her primary roles. Later, she undertook the job of getting the maternal/child clinic started. I was about to take a load of clinic and feeding center employees home from the party that evening. We had borrowed a pickup from the Catholic Services unit. I was standing along the street in the dark, waiting for the women to climb onto the truck. As we were about to leave, a little boy—I guessed about eight or nine years old—was standing at my elbow and said, "Bossman, could you help me with my troubles?" Since I was just ready to leave, I said yes, and told him to get in the truck. The women were cheerful and noisy as we drove. After nearly everyone was off, I told Christina, one of the charge nurses at the feeding center, how it had come about that I had the little boy with me. When we got to her place, we found out that his mother was killed by Doe's soldiers the previous summer. He said his name was Michael. His father was supposed to be in Bassa County, but he hadn't heard from him since his mother's death. He was existing by begging and stealing. He mostly slept in doorways of boarded-up shops or in abandoned cars.

Getting no suggested solution from Christina, I took him home. After giving him something to eat, Margaret Eaton, Susan, and I discussed the options. We all agreed that taking him to Dorothy was the thing to do. Dorothy was a lady who had a small house on the beach at Mamba Point, just below the United States Embassy. During the fall and winter of 1990, when the fighting and starvation was at its worst, children would hide in the rocks below the embassy. During the day, they would scrounge for food. Any cooking done was in the rocks late in the day. They also slept there at night. Dorothy got involved by getting some of the Marines at the embassy to throw small packages of food and rice across the fence to her. It wasn't long before she had over a hundred children that she was providing for in one way or another. The small food packages had become large bags of rice.

It was ten PM before we got Michael to Dorothy's place. Several of the older boys were still cleaning up and washing dishes. Dorothy's reply to our request was, "Boys, you just got another brother." One of the boys got soap and water for a bath. The boy we had brought was filthy and in rags. At the time we were there, she had 110 children. Dr. Dustin, from the U.S. Embassy, was helping her with the children who were sick. When he left for home, I started stopping by twice a week to see several of the children that had TB. The unofficial name for Dorothy's place among the relief workers was "The Good Samaritan Orphanage."

On another occasion, a woman came to Juanita Shenk who was visiting at our apartment one evening. The woman had several small children and a new-born set of twins. The staff took her and the children back to Bushrod Island with a supply of food.

The following are journal accounts of people slipping through rebel lines into the city at night:

Today I saw three women who slipped into the city during the night. These people are often completely destitute. The feeding program is designed to catch everyone who has a place to stay. Unless the new people arrive just before the first of the month, they often have a long wait to get on the food dispersement rolls. With 750,000 people in a place with a normal population half that size, finding a place to call home is practically impossible. All three of the women lost children to the war—two of them lost their husbands. All the children are sick. One of the infants went to the Swedish Hospital, another to our feeding center. With no place to go and no food allowance, it is difficult to know what to do with these people. Often we just give them Liberian money to allow time to get them into the regular feeding program.

The March 23 journal entry talked of a 13-year-old boy and our ambulance service: The boy weighed 50 pounds. His father carried him most of the way to the Marshall Clinic this morning. A man with a wheelbarrow pushed him the last several miles. Large, what we used to call "cement" wheelbarrows were frequently used to bring patients to the clinic. It seemed like an efficient ambulance service. It was also cheap. The boy had been separated from his parents the previous four or five months. He had bloody dysentery with a barely readable blood pressure. We kept him on the bedpan while he received two liters of 5% dextrose in normal saline. He was too weak to talk; his eyes wouldn't focus. A single dose of Cipro and Bismuth worked near miracles in these children. This patient probably wouldn't have survived without this and IV fluids.

More March 23 notes: Palm trees were a problem to several patients today. A twelve-year-old boy was climbing a coconut palm and fell, fracturing a knee cap. Later in the day a man came in, afraid he had been bitten by a green mamba (snake). He had climbed a coconut palm to pick coconuts. One can only climb to the leafy growth

"we learned to live with the unexpected"

at the top and at that point one has to reach around, to the center pod, to pick the coconuts. When he did this, he felt a sting-like pain, and was afraid he had been bitten by a snake. The green mamba has a deadly bite and is known to hide in coconut palms to wait for prey. In this case, there was no evidence of a bite. The main proof that the man wasn't bitten was that the patient was alive.

This afternoon I took a walk downtown. More things are available on the street. Very little is sold in conventional stores. Most of the stores that weren't destroyed are still locked and boarded up. A sad commentary we see daily is the abundance of American cigarettes for sale on the street. The streets are full of little children selling one or two cigarettes at a time. I am told by people who lived through it, that cigarettes remained in good supply at the time thousands were starving last summer and fall. On a walk on the beach it is not unusual to find bones from the burials of the previous fall and summer.

March 28: I saw eleven people who arrived in the past 48 hours. Here at the Marshall Clinic, the rebel lines are only five miles away across the St. Paul River. Fighting has been increasing because of competition for food and other resources. Some of the new arrivals have stories of having to hide in the bush for several days before they get a chance to slip across. On top of this, I inherited a twelve-day-old infant. Two young men came to the clinic this pm asking me to go to a place along the St. Paul River where an old man has a baby that is sure to starve. The story was that the mother of the child was psychotic. During the fighting last summer, two of the mother's sisters and one brother were killed. She was raped by the soldiers and had given birth to the new baby twelve days ago. She had been acting strange before the baby was born. Since the baby was born, she has stayed out in the bush and only occasionally shows herself.

After I finished at the clinic, the two men and I went to the house. I had the four-wheel drive vehicle or it would have been a long walk. The baby was alone with the grandfather. He said his wife died of a broken heart after their children were killed. The baby had been getting only "bush tea." It looked like ordinary tea. The baby was weak and underweight but seemed alert. When the grandfather insisted, I agreed to take the baby back to Monrovia with me. The mother showed herself just momentarily before we left. I told the grandfather that we would have someone stay in touch with him.

Going back, I cradled the baby in my arm. There were eight military check points I had to pass going to and from the clinic. By then, most of the soldiers knew me and the vehicle. They fussed over the baby just like a mother. I took him to Swedish Hospital where I was acquainted with several of the nurses from a get-together at the U.S. Embassy the previous Friday night. The nurses took us in and proceeded to give me an education. One of the nurses took me to the sidewalk entrance where a long line of patients were waiting to be seen. She walked down the line until she got to a woman with a small healthy-looking child. After a little discussion, the mother came with us. A few minutes later, my baby—we called him Billy—was breast-feeding. A week later, he had gained several pounds. He was breast-feeding from as many as four different mothers.

March 29: It's been a frustrating morning—we are running out of drugs daily. Just a few simple lab supplies that are missing would let us do some sorely needed tests. After thinking on this, I decided to try getting a message to Church World Services New York or to Mennonite Board of Missions in Elkhart. With no mail or telephone service, the two flights each week from Freetown are the only contacts to the outside world. At mid-morning, I left the clinic and went to the airport with a prepared list of our needs. Two men that looked like possibilities were leaving on this day's flight. I went to the likeliest one and told him my needs. His name was Tom Bridges and he was with the U.S. State Department. He assured me he would get my message delivered.

P.S. We got the requested supplies in eight days. The shipment included a large number of other necessary supplies.

March 31: I attended the Episcopal church today. The service was more formal and ritualistic than the Protestant congregations I had worshipped with in Monrovia. Liberian President Amos Sawyer and the U.S. Ambassador were the last two signatures on the guest register above mine. They sat in the pew directly in front of me.

April 10: Ralph Royer arrived from Freetown with Willis Logan and Samuel Pieh. Ralph will assume the role of logician for our unit. In addition to our health care projects, cws (Church World Services) is financing several agricultural projects with a resource worker and supplies. Ralph took overall responsibility for those projects. He will also be seeing to the unit's food and housing needs.

April 13: A new TB patient, a little seven-year-old girl, was seen today. A little later, a mother brought her six-year-old son in with a hemoglobin of 3.5 and hematocrit of 14%. He was also severely dehydrated. He couldn't walk and wouldn't eat. His primary problem appeared to be malnutrition with malaria. This city of 750,000 people has less than one hundred hospital beds. Earlier, several malignancies we had tried to get care for were turned away. We were told that they would probably die anyway. When I decided to give this little boy a blood transfusion we ran into problems. The hospitals refused our request for a type and cross match. We told them we didn't want him admitted, but just wanted the type and cross match done. We promised to supply the donor. When this fell on deaf ears, I went to the hospital myself. By going straight to the lab, in my best don't-you-dare-refuse-me tone, I got what I wanted. Juanita ended up donating a unit of blood and the little fellow got his transfusion. We subsequently treated the malaria. Six weeks later he came to the clinic and wasn't recognized because of his healthy appearance. His mother claimed that his father was a famous Liberian soccer player.

April 14: One Sunday morning, our breakfast was interrupted by one of our neighbor's house boys. He had a one inch laceration across his left eyelid. A fragment of a fluorescent light bulb had fallen on him. Juanita helped clean and suture the wound.

April 18: Today I saw a 30-year-old man with paralysis of his right forearm and hand. He was caught by rebel soldiers a week earlier. They had tied his arms behind his back just above the elbows. He was tied up so tightly and for so long that he suffered nerve damage. The arm was still edematous with the rope indentation and burns present. The day after he was tied up, passers-by heard him calling for help and released him. There wasn't much to do for him. I told him recovery often takes a number of months.

Two of the Swedish Hospital nurses came to the clinic to see if I could help them contact the St. Paul River baby's grandfather. They had found two ladies who wanted to adopt the baby.

April 20: Since rebel raids into Sierra Leone, all commercial flights from Freetown have been stopped.

April 25: The big news today is the arrival of Howard and Ruth Miller from Lowville, New York, and of Kelly Jewett from Minnesota. Howard and Ruth are Registered Nurses. Kelly graduated from medical school this spring. At the Marshall Clinic, one of the men diagnosed with TB a month ago was seen again today. His progress was remarkable. He asked if he could wash our vehicle each clinic day. I suspected that he wanted to be paid, but found out that wasn't the case.

P.S. He did this faithfully throughout the rest of the time

I served at the clinic. The new staff arrivals were very able and willing workers. They provided a needed spark to the unit.

April 27: This morning, I saw a nine-year-old girl that, from what we can piece together, walked about 65 miles, partly through the bush the last four days. She arrived with open wounds and sores on her legs. Five days earlier, her family awoke at night with shooting taking place around them. Her parents grabbed the younger children and told her to run. They all got separated in the bush. She continued walking through the night until she came to a road. She apparently slept or at least rested there until other refugees came along. These people shared what food they had with her. From there, she was able to stay with others until she arrived at the checkpoint in front of the Marshall Clinic. From her description of the road and bridges she crossed, our staff figured she walked here from somewhere in Bomi County.

Five break-ins, robberies, and muggings have taken place in our part of the city the past several days. People were killed in two of them. Most of the people involved were members of foreign service organizations. I talked to Donald Showalter from Allegheny County, Virginia, today. He is in charge of security for the U.S. Embassy and their buildings, including our apartment. He discouraged us from moving to private housing.

April 29: This week, one of the small newsletters available on the streets reported that the Freeport area, where ships dock, was open to the public again. Earlier, when I had gone to the docks to visit the Firestone ship's captain, I had to go through a lot of red tape just to get to the port area. At the time, I was trying to find a way to arrange for food shipments and other aid supplies from the States. The captain told me that Firestone Rubber Company would provide free freight to Monrovia for cargo containers shipped by voluntary aide agencies. The agency's containers would need to be loaded and ready for shipment from the Port of Baltimore. Before the war, round trips from Baltimore to Monrovia were made about every six weeks. Firestone was planning to resume the route on a reduced schedule as demand and safety allowed. Because of their large rubber plantations, Firestone had a large pre-war presence in Liberia. Our arrangement didn't work out because we lacked communication capabilities to coordinate shipments. By the time communication capabilities were available, the scheduled ships were canceled.

Today, I had a different reason to visit the docks. One of my Lebanese friends who operated a freight brokerage business told me that there might be some short term travel possibilities on one of the ships plying the ports along the West African coast. He told me a number of small freighters were plying the ports again from Dakar, Senegal, to Lagos, Nigeria, on a continuous basis. Their itinerary brought them back to Monrovia every five to fifteen days, depending on safety and weather. He also told me that I could possibly get on a smaller fishing vessel that stayed out for shorter periods of time. I was encouraged to take up to a week's leave in a guest house in Freetown, Sierra Leone, during my stay in Liberia.

Since I wasn't interested in any more experiences in Freetown, the sailing possibilities sounded attractive.

I was stopped several times for identification, but there were no security searches today. Except for one large freighter unloading rice, there was only one other vessel at the docks. It turned out to be a Greek fishing trawler. I soon had the attention of one of the crew members. By sign language and a few commonly understood words, they quickly caught on that I wanted to see the man in charge. Three of the crew escorted me to the captain's quarters. He was very accommodating. He spoke fluent English, and invited me to stay for lunch. We had a nice visit over a sandwich and cold coke, which was a treat. The captain informed me that the ship specialized in catching lobsters, large shrimp and a few other specialty sea foods. The crew processed the catch on board and once the freezers were full, they headed back to Greece. When I left, the captain presented me with a five pound box of jumbo shrimp. The shrimp were all from six to seven inches long when we measured them later.

The captain of the Greek ship told me that Monrovia was one of the ports that they used for supplies and fuel before the war. The ship's present problem was mechanical and they would have to lay over for parts. I left the dock after a pleasant lunch and visit, but without any ship-junket possibilities.

From the Greek ship, I walked about one hundred yards to a large mahogany logging yard. There, I watched several men in various stages of hewing and burning out logs to make boats. I took several pictures and was about to leave when a soldier with a rifle confronted me. Since he spoke only French, we couldn't communicate. He motioned with his rifle for me to accompany him. He led me around several fences to an old building where his superior officer sat outside the door on an old box. Here, they tried to get me to turn over my backpack, billfold, and camera. The officer knew just enough English for me to realize that they were accusing me of taking pictures of a military unit without permission. With as much confidence as I could muster, I demanded to be taken to their commanding officer. After some consideration, the soldiers complied with my request. The commanding officer didn't speak English either, but something told me he spoke German. When I addressed him in that language, his attitude immediately softened. Just a few words of explanation and I was being escorted to the camp gates. As I left, I could hear him loudly chastising the soldiers who had intercepted me.

May 2: Ralph brought me a telex notifying me of Grandmother Coblentz's death.

May 4: We had dinner at Dr. Dustin's house on the embassy grounds. Our meal included the jumbo shrimp I got at the port last week. All our people were there along with the embassy security chief and military attache. We are beginning to see signs of the rainy season, with daily rain.

From mid-May: Howard, Ralph, and I played in the embassy tennis tournament. I played with a Swede. We won our first match but ended up losing to the tournament winner. Ralph and his partner did well.

I need to mention a few of the lighter side events that took place, too. The last 30 days were more relaxed. I continued to see a general improvement in nutrition. With their improved appearance, I felt freer to ask patients and their families if I could take their pictures. A family with identical three-year-old triplet boys came to see me in May. They were all well-nourished with the exception of a younger sister who was ill with malaria. The boys' names were Shadrach, Meshach, and Abednego. One of the staff took a picture of me holding the three boys.

At a time when I needed a haircut, a young man on a downtown sidewalk caught my attention. On my way home from the clinic I noticed his sign. It turned out to be quite an experience. I asked a few questions about his skills and told him to go ahead. He was no sooner started when he began bragging to his friends about his experiences giving "bossman" haircuts. His colorful description quickly brought me to the conclusion that the only white men's hair he had ever cut were U.S. Marines. By that time, reconsidering my decision was too late. I never did find out if he actually cut hair for some of the Marines, but I do know that I got a crew-cut.

During the first four to six weeks in Monrovia there were no fruits, vegetables, or meats available. This somewhat restricted diet was alleviated a little the third week after my arrival in Monrovia. The U.S. Embassy opened their commissary each Friday night to aide workers in the city. The cheeseburger and coke I had that first night, was, to say the least, delightful. During this period, Dr. Dustin invited me to lunch at his house at the embassy compound. I told him how I appreciated the meal. When he inquired about our food sources, I told him that other than rice, we had limited supplies. After lunch, he took me out to several large mango trees on the embassy grounds. There, we filled several plastic bags with mangos. They were greatly appreciated back at our unit.

One day after lunch, I took a slide to the embassy medical office to do an acid-fast stain. While there, Bob Parnell, the military attache, asked me to go to the office of Mike Nelson, the security chief. A short while later I had a U.S. Embassy staff pass. Dr. Dustin had told me earlier that he would try to arrange this. The embassy was helpful by letting me use their facility for things we couldn't do or for supplies we didn't have. On several occasions I was able to return the favor. Being able to bypass the embassy clearance process was a relief. The pass allowed me to use the pool, the tennis courts, the restaurant, and the commissary.

Conventional wisdom often didn't hold in Monrovia. Gasoline was rationed to aide agencies through the United Nations' office. During the worst times the U.N. charged us twelve U.S. dollars per gallon. After the price dropped to six dollars per gallon, street vendors set up shop. All it took for them to go into business was a container to hold the gasoline. Most of the vendors had five gallon cans, and in some cases one gallon glass or plastic jugs held the vendor's entire inventory.

Dr. Reed, the new embassy doctor, was very helpful. On several occasions I was able to get badly needed medicines and supplies that were not available anywhere else in Monrovia. In one instance, a young English aide worker had a seizure on the plane from Freetown to Monrovia. The only supply of anti-seizure medication in Monrovia was in the embassy medical office.

Just as when I came to Liberia, leaving was also a challenge. Twice-a-week flights to Abidjan, Ivory Coast, had just been instituted. Because the Freetown-to-London flights were stopped earlier, I had no valid ticket back to Europe. A call to British Air informed me that I had to fly their airline from Abidjan or have my ticket assigned to another airline. After arriving in Abidjan, the ticket agent told me that if I wanted to fly another airline, I would have to go to the downtown British Air office and get my ticket endorsed. The next British Air flight would require a two days' wait in the "restricted customs" section of the airport. With no visa for the Ivory Coast, I couldn't legally leave the airport.

When my attempts to acquire a visa led nowhere, I took a seat in the customs section and watched people coming and going. The taxi stop to pick up and drop off passengers was in open view. An hour's sitting was enough to assure me that I didn't want to wait another thirty-five hours. The hour's watching showed that the security guards were making their rounds of the area in a predictable pattern. I reached a decision. If a few short excursions just past the security gate brought no response, I would proceed through the gate and flag a taxi. If that didn't work, I would try the "oh-dumb-me" approach.

As people departed in taxis, I saw that just a few seconds elapsed from the time it took to go from the terminal exit gate to the curb and a waiting taxi. Fifteen minutes later, as I walked through the gate, I thought of Father's admonition to always walk like you're going somewhere. A large modern divided four-lane highway served as egress for the airport. Stately rows of palm trees lined its grass divider strip. Just seconds later as we left the airport grounds, my heart jumped into my throat when we were stopped by a military policeman. Since the soldier and cab driver spoke only French, I couldn't understand what was being said. About this time though, the situation became self-explanatory. Traffic was stopped in both directions to allow a shepherd to herd a large flock of sheep across the roadway.

A short ride later, I was in the downtown British Air office. It took only a few minutes to get their endorsement for Air Afrique. From there, I was sent to the Air Afrique office to get a ticket for Paris. Two hours later, we were on our way to Europe. The flight went through Niamey, Niger, and Marseille, France, to Paris. There I changed to a United flight to Washington DC.

An amusing thing happened in Paris. I visited with a lady from Pompano Beach, Florida. She had just arrived from London and had given me her *Herald Tribune* and *London Times*. When she got up for her plane, she reached out to shake hands. Without thinking, I did a finger-snap handshake like the Liberians do. It startled both of us. She found my explanation amusing and said she wanted to try it on a Lebanese friend with Liberian connections.

The first person I saw after coming through customs in Washington DC, was Andrew sitting on Mark's shoulders. Carol, Mary, Lois, and Travis were there to greet me, too. Coming back to the Shenandoah Valley was a wonderful homecoming.

As I am writing about these experiences in Liberia in 1991, intense fighting has erupted again in Monrovia. I would like to go back to help with the orphaned children if it becomes safe. There are several staff members at our clinics I still wonder about. One was a young South African political refugee who was a third-year medical student in Monrovia when the war broke out. He had no passport to get back to South Africa. With the political changes there I wonder if he's been able to return.

A New Beginning

IN LATE MARCH 1990, I HAD COME TO OHIO TO ATTEND MY son David's wedding. During the trip, I stopped by the emergency room at Joel Pomerene Hospital. While visiting with the staff, I chanced to see LaVina Miller, one of the part time O.R. nurses. Not getting to talk to her, I asked one of the other nurses if she would send me LaVina's address and phone number. I knew LaVina only briefly from my work there earlier. She had started work in the spring of 1989, soon after I did. She was here temporarily, from Goshen, Indiana, to help care for her father who had had a stroke. When I didn't hear from the nurse by late April, I called information and got LaVina's sister's number and under the pretext of business interests, I got LaVina's telephone number. A phone call followed to ask LaVina for permission to exchange letters. We exchanged letters three or four times over the next six months. This exchange came to an end when she went to Thailand in late 1990, and I went to Liberia during the first part of 1991.

On my return from Liberia I worked around the farm in Virginia for several weeks. Subsequently, I returned to Ohio and accepted a temporary invitation to move in with my parents. Emergency room duties in Shelby, Bucyrus, Napoleon, Mount Vernon, and Millersburg, Ohio, kept me fully occupied. By late fall, my work was confined to Joel Pomerene Hospital in Millersburg. On my days off, Father and I visited many old friends and neighbors. We visited two of the old one-room school sites he attended 75 years earlier. Getting the driving horse harnessed and hitched for short trips in the neighborhood was no different than it was forty years earlier. In the fall, we went to Missouri to visit my brother Lester and his family. My brother Eli's son, Kevin, went along to help drive. Father's health was failing some, but he was able to enjoy this leisurely trip.

In early December, in one of the hospital corridors I chanced to meet Vivian Wolf, head nurse in surgery. She told me that LaVina Miller was being offered the Director of Nursing position at Joel Pomerene Hospital after she returned to the states from her year of voluntary service in Thailand. This bit of news got me back to mulling over how single living was going for me. It was now over two years since Lovina's death. It appeared that I was getting into a comfort zone where any kind of romantic involvement seemed too risky. Up until this time, the issue was avoided by keeping my relationships platonic and at arm's length.

In December, LaVina accepted the hospital position. In January 1992 she started work. A few days later, after getting back from a medical seminar, I sent her a flower arrangement. To make this gesture appear strictly professional, a "Welcome back to Joel Pomerene" card was included. This was followed up with a short visit in her office for a personal welcome. From the

Wayne & LaVina

moment she answered my knock with, "come in," I realized that something was brewing. My response and feelings were becoming uncharacteristic. Was I experiencing butterflies? Surely this quivery feeling in my stomach doesn't happen to a mature fifty-five year old doctor.

The next week, between bouts of feeling like a blundering sixteen year old, I invited her out to dinner. From this start, our relationship blossomed into several months of courtship. We were soon at the point where some decision making was required. My parents were the first in the family that I told about this budding relationship. Father was interested in who she was. With what information I knew, he filled in what he knew of her genealogy. I could tell her Holmes County roots pleased him. He was impressed with her years of voluntary service in Haiti and more recently in Thailand. His acceptance and regard for LaVina was reassuring to me. The next week he surprised me with a family tree chart of her ancestors.

It took several months to work through the, do-I-make-a-serious-commitment-or-jump-ship, question. Is it realistic to expect to integrate a previous thirty-year-marriage experience into another relationship? Will my children and grandchildren approve? When our initial visit to my family in Virginia went well, we continued our relationship. The following month of July I spent at home in Virginia. During this time, I reached a decision to propose marriage to LaVina. If she didn't agree, I would accept her decision as the right one. When she accepted, we arranged for several pastoral counseling sessions. When no apparent red flags were raised, we went ahead with plans for a November wedding. In September, we bought a home north of Millersburg. It needed a lot of work that family members helped us with. After the wedding, we went on a honeymoon cruise in the Caribbean.

Any reservations I had about remarriage have long since dissipated. The children and grandchildren have accepted LaVina well. She appears to have been made for instant grandmothering. Her three year contract as Director of Nursing was completed in January 1995. Following several months of part-time work, she became a full-time homemaker. Her coming into my life has been a godsend.

The Children
In Later Years

T HE CHILDREN WENT TO EASTERN MENNONITE HIGH
School from grade seven to grade twelve. In the summer
between school terms, David, with the others helping, started
raising produce in our river bottom. He raised tomatoes, sweet
corn, and cucumbers, but hybrid cantaloupes were the main
crop. In his most productive year, he sold twenty thousand cantaloupes. Most of the produce was sold through local super-
markets. The children also had a produce stand in the town of
Weyers Cave. During the peak season each summer, they hauled
several loads to Ohio.

David also ran a firewood business during the energy crisis
years. After high school, he continued the produce and wood
business while attending Blue Ridge Community College and
Eastern Mennonite College. Since his graduation from Eastern
Mennonite College in 1986, he has been teaching school in
Ohio. In 1990, David married Mary Yoder, daughter of Edna

and Eli Yoder. Mary's father is deceased. David and Mary live in Sugarcreek, Ohio, with their daughter Rachel and son Aaron. Their daughter, Abigail, was born since beginning these recollections.

In his last year in high school, I tried to help Mark with decisions about furthering his years of schooling versus starting work right away. The children all had work experiences. During their high school years, they all milked at one time or another for several of the larger dairy farms in our neighborhood. They also helped with the farm work at home.

During Christmas vacation in Mark's senior year, we decided to dabble in a business venture. We had access to an unlimited number of fireplace mats that we could buy at a large discount because of minor cosmetic defects. After deciding to go ahead with the venture, we headed north towards Cumberland, Maryland, with a truckload of mats. Any stove or fireplace outlets we came across were fair game. The day was going fairly well sales-wise when another one of those embarrassing moments in my life took place.

Just outside Waynesboro, Pennsylvania, we stopped at a wood stove and fireplace outlet. The owner seemed interested but I thought he needed just a little nudge. "Ah," I thought, "he thinks they aren't strong enough." My way of demonstrating their strength was a disaster. I put the end of a five-by-two foot mat on a lower stair step and jumped on the middle, promptly breaking it in two. I assured the store owner that something had to be wrong, and before Mark could stop me, I broke another mat perfectly down the middle. I noticed that Mark looked concerned with the first one, but he, and the potential buyer, were practically rolling on the floor in laughter by the time I broke the second one. With laughter, the man told us he felt sorry for me and bought ten mats—the biggest sale of the day. When I had the mats demonstrated to me at the plant a year earlier, the mats had metal bars in them for stiffening. Mark was aware that the factory had changed the mats to fiberglass reinforcement. I, obviously, wasn't. We didn't tell the store owner that I was a physician. In spite of incidents like this, our children still all claim me as their father. The above incident, I am sure, had something to do with Mark choosing poultry farming and construction as his primary occupation.

Mark started to work for a construction firm right out of high school. He worked at this trade until his marriage in 1985. His wife, Carol, is the daughter of Bob and Miriam Shenk of Harrisonburg, Virginia. Bob owned the Honda motorcycle and equipment dealership in Harrisonburg for many years. The Shenks also raised poultry during more recent years. Mark always had an interest in farming. After Mark and Carol were married, they lived in a mobile home on the Shenk farm. Here they raised broilers under an agreement with his father-in-law while Mark continued his full-time construction work. This poultry raising experience led Mark and Carol to plan for their own poultry operation. In 1988, they bought a forty-two acre property near the Weyers Cave airport. It was a property Lovina and I had owned for several years. They now have two tom turkey houses and a small herd of beef cattle. In 1995, they moved into a new house that Mark, with the help of several of his friends, built himself. Four little boys, Andrew, Travis, Tyler, and Doyle complete this Weaver household.

Mary, our oldest daughter, attended Blue Ridge Community College. She has been working at Rockingham Memorial Hospital since graduating from an R.N. nursing program. She is presently working as an assistant floor manager while working on a B.S. degree in nursing. Mary married Greg Lam of Mount Solon, Virginia, in April, 1993. He is the son of Sam and Betty

Lam. Greg works in the business office of a large custom metal fabricating shop in Bridgewater, Virginia. They bought the home place on the river and twenty acres of land. Mary has artistic talents that are waiting for the right time. Their first child, Garrett Monroe, was born June 5, 1996, the week I am writing this.

Lois, our youngest daughter, lives near Mark, between Weyers Cave and Grottoes. At the present time, Mark is building a new house for Lois on several acres of land from off the home place. Mark lives about seven miles from the home place. After high school, Lois went to James Madison University. Despite good grades and starting on the varsity volleyball team, she became disenchanted with school. She wanted to do a term of voluntary service with one of the Mennonite Mission programs. She served in an inner-city day care center in Louisville, Kentucky, for a year. After that, she worked as a secretary and receptionist in a wholesale business in Harrisonburg until her mother's illness. Since her break from work to help care for her mother, she has been working for a retail business in Dayton, Virginia, that is owned and operated by Oren and Margaret Heatwole. She is one of the assistant managers in the business at the present time.

My Father

MY FATHER WAS THE MOST SIGNIFICANT ROLE MODEL IN MY life. I was reminded of this when I lived with my parents from July 1991 until April 1992. Getting reunited after 28 years out of state was an enjoyable experience. Eating Mother's cooking and getting used to living without telephones and electricity again re-established my roots. We spent hours talking about my father's Amish genealogy work. After his seventy-fifth birthday, he spent a greater portion of his time studying Amish history and family lines. Over this period, he made approximately two hundred family tree charts for people with Amish roots. He seemed to know some bit of interesting background information about nearly every Amish family line in Holmes County. In 1967, Father had a misfortune he struggled with until his death. Their home was destroyed by fire. In it, he lost 37 years of personal diaries and 35 years of his own father's diaries—a loss not measurable in dollars. This included diaries from his grandfa-

Monroe A. Weaver

Elizabeth Schlabach Weaver

ther. Together, they had daily diaries from 1900 or earlier. At the time of his death in 1993, he had accumulated another 25 years of diaries. Father wrote a weekly article for the *Sugarcreek Budget* for many years. *The Budget* is a weekly newspaper with community news coverage of the Amish and more conservative Mennonite settlements throughout the country and around the world.

For years he had talked about visiting "the old country." In the mid-seventies he first started planning seriously towards this goal. Carl Yoder, a dentist, and Paul Hummel, a Mennonite pastor, both from Holmes County, helped him make contacts in Germany. This was the same Paul Hummel that provided the impetus for my medical career. After several years of communication by mail with these people, Father realized the need for a resource person in Switzerland. In 1977, the summer before his anticipated trip, my father came up with a unique way to find such a person. On his way to the Sugarcreek Livestock auction he stopped at Der Dutchman restaurant in Walnut Creek, Ohio. There he went through their guest book until he found a Switzerland address. The first name he found was Hans Brechbühler from Burgdorf, Switzerland. A letter to Hans started an exchange of information that led to Father staying with the Brechbühlers in Switzerland the next year. Hans, in return, has visited Father here in the States six or seven times over the last fifteen years.

Later in 1977, Father answered an ad in the *Sugarcreek Budget* advertising a six-week tour of Europe. It provided for ship travel for those who didn't want to travel by air. Not long after he signed up for the tour came the armchair preparation phase with maps, books, and fellow travelers. He always claimed this part of the trip was as much fun as the journey itself. Finally, on April 30, 1978, he left on a chartered bus for New

York City. There were twenty people in the group. With the exception of several Old Order Mennonites, the travelers were all Amish. At 7:00 PM the same day, the Queen Elizabeth II pulled anchor and sailed for Europe. For details of the ocean voyage and European tour through Father's eyes, read his small book, *Amish Europe and Holy Land Tour via Queen Elizabeth II.* The book is a delightful description of detail that is vintage— my father.

He liked to tell of events in his childhood. The end of World War I was celebrated with early dismissal from school and the ringing of school and church bells. He recalled the time when there were no paved roads throughout the county. As a young boy, he went along when an Amish family moved north to Wayne County. He was with a group of boys who drove the cattle and horses. They crossed State Route 62 and State Route 250. Both were gravel roads at the time. Father and his first cousin, Emanuel Mullet, got their team stuck in the mud on State Route 62 between Winesburg and Wilmot, Ohio, one spring. They had gone to pick up a load of empty egg crates. On the way home, one of the horses got stuck in the mud. They had to get help from another team to pull the horse out. That spring, Father was ten and Emanuel was nine.

Father recalled being told that his great-grandfather, Benjamin Weaver, had one of the first windmills to pump water. This modern convenience caused some in the community to voice objections. A few went as far as taking detours to avoid passing the windmill. An elderly woman in the community was supposed to have said, "*Now vella mere Gott noch macha vassa bumpa*" ("Now we even want to make God pump the water"). Father's comment regarding this was, he didn't see how anyone could be against windmills. On the other hand, he reminded me that change isn't always the same thing as progress. We discussed how it came about that the Amish accepted railroad transportation when it first became available. Many of the Amish came to the midwest from the eastern states by train. Earlier, many Mennonite and Amish immigrants came to Ohio via the Erie Canal system. Prior to that, they came by foot, horseback, or wagon.

For a man with a horse and buggy, Father got around a lot. He visited all the lower 48 states and Canada and Mexico. He took a passenger train to the west coast with some of his grandchildren in the '70s. In later years, his travels beyond five or ten miles were usually by automobile or van. He considered his trip to Europe on the Queen Elizabeth II the highlight of his travel experiences. Father liked history and geography trivia questions. Friends who visited looked forward to these tidbits of information. Some came in a did-you-know format. For example: Did you know that President Hoover was born in Germany? At other times, you could expect a little pop quiz. An example: Where would you hit South America if you traveled straight south from Cleveland, Ohio? The answer—you miss it on the Pacific side—was a surprise to most.

Father had a wide variety of interests. Some were a little unusual. Sometime during the '70s, he got interested in carrier pigeons. It wasn't long before he had several hatchlings. Before the pigeons were mature enough to be released, he built a special pigeon shelter that protected the birds from wild and domestic predators. The pigeons could come and go at will from this enclosure. During the time he waited for the carrier pigeons to mature, Father bought some tumbler pigeons. We were entertained with their flying antics.

In the following years, detailed reports of Father's carrier pigeon releases reached us in Virginia. We anticipated witnessing a release on one of my parents' visits to our home in Virginia.

The release from our house never came about because Father never had any birds ready at the right time. I do recall that several pairs were released in Indiana, and at a later time, in Pennsylvania. On each of these occasions, only one bird of the pair returned to their Ohio origins. At the time of this writing, three years after my father's death, Mother tells me the pigeon shelter is still the home for offspring of the original pigeons Father bought.

Benjamin Weaver 1838-1919

Anna Gerber 1841-1913

John N. Weaver 1837-1918

Barbara Miller 1838-1919

Isaac Hershberger Jr. P-1817-1888-HO

Anna Hershberger 1824-1891

Dan C. Yoder (M1) P-1824-1855-P

Catherine Hochstetler P-1828-1821-P

Jacob J. Ashlabach 1836-1919

Mary Miller 1830-1906

Solomon Miller 1816-1910

Mary Brenneman (G) 1812-1895-HO

Samuel D. Yoder P-1827-1908-HO

Elizabeth Beachy SP-1821-1873

Daniel Conrad 1837-1923

Susanna Hershberger 1837-1906

One of Father's Genealogy Charts Showing Six Generations

Wayne M. Weaver
7-3-37-

Monroe A. Weaver
7-7-1909-
M-1-14-1934

Elizabeth Schlabach
5-24-1913-

Atlee A. Weaver
7-14-1885 — 2-2-1961
M-2-24-1907

Fannie Hengerd
10-17-1884 — 1-21-1962

Daniel G. Schlabach
3-15-1880 — 5-11-1934
M-2-8-1906

Amanda Yoder
3-11-1886 — 2-2-1944

Emanuel B. Weaver (M1)
4-6-1864 — 3-31-1948

Amanda J. Weaver
11-15-1868 — 6-6-1889

Isaac Hengerd Jr.
6-25-1860 — 3-24-1931

Barbara Yoder
P-7-15-1858 — 5-10-1931

Eli D. Schlabach
11-9-1856 — 7-3-1926

Magdalena Miller
1-2-1846 — 12-31-1916

Abraham S. Yoder
M4-7-4-1859 — 4-24-1934

Mattie Oswald
11-5-1861 — 2-20-1926

One of Father's Genealogy Charts Showing Six Generations

Looking At Our Roots

ON AUGUST 9, 1993, LAVINA AND I LEFT FOR A FOUR-WEEK trip to Europe. We had a ten-day itinerary planned before we were to meet a tour group and attend the three-hundredth anniversary of the Swiss Brethren division that gave rise to the Amish. From Washington DC, we flew to Paris where we spent several days touring the city. The usual Paris sights included the Louvre, the Seine on an evening cruise, the Eiffel Tower, and the Notre Dame Cathedral. We patronized and enjoyed the sidewalk cafes along the Champ Élysées. On a leisurely stroll along this street, we met William Talbot and his wife from my former home in Virginia. Dr. Talbot is a retired pathologist from Rockingham Memorial Hospital in Harrisonburg. A short walk from our hotel, followed by a fifteen minute train ride, took us to the Palace of Versailles and its gardens. Here the size, quality, and quantity of everything was so opulent that it dulled the senses. The palace fit the image of Louis XIV that one sees in paintings. Later the same day, we took a train to Lyon. At 150 miles an hour, it wasn't a long journey. A train change in Lyon took us across the Jura Mountains to Bern, Switzerland.

The next morning, Hans Brechbühler met us at the hotel. After we had our car rented, Hans showed us parts of the city. He tried to take us to places he and Father had visited. He often reminded us while eating that they had eaten there too. He accompanied us on a tour covering things of general interest as well as Anabaptist history. We spent four days together in perfect weather. The Emmental River valley and the surrounding

Hans Brechbühler

countryside is where the largest part of our Amish ancestors came from. Many of our outings passed home after home with present day American Amish and Mennonite names. He showed us the farm where the Amish Yoder family originated. The farm is called "Yoder Hübel" (Yoder's Hill). Yoders are first recorded as living there in 1260 AD.

On our last day with Hans, we went to Zurich. This was the city where the Anabaptist movement started, in 1525. He took us to the places historically connected to the movement's start. Zurich was the canton where our immigrant ancestor, Jacob Weaver, was allegedly born. Later, we would visit the Palatinate region where he and his cousin Christian are thought to have left from for America. In the evening, Hans left us at our hotel and caught a train back to Burgdorf. He has a railroad pass that gives him free travel all over Switzerland. The next morning we caught a train for Vienna, Austria. It took us through Innsbruck and Salzburg. This must be one of the most picturesque train rides in the world. Vienna is an interesting old city. All through the trip we kept being reminded that what is called "old" in the States is not considered old in Europe. When we talk of a building that is one or two hundred years old, they talk of one that is five hundred or a thousand years old. We visited museums and several palaces the first day. The first evening we ate in a revolving restaurant on top of a tall tower along the Danube River.

At the Schönbrunn Palace we had an interesting experience. As we came into the receiving room on a tour of the Palace, the far wall displayed a large oil painting. In the painting, standing on the right side, was a lady dressed like my grandmother did when I was a child. The woman in the painting wore a head covering and a dark cape dress. The painting was from, I believe, about 1660. A second interesting thing in the painting was the depiction of a crowded marketplace. In a conspicuous place to the left and in front of the lady was an average sized table, but with one exception. Its top was about four feet off the ground. Around the table, leaning on an elbow with their head in hand, were several men. Beside one man was a small monkey picking fleas out of the man's hair. We were told that this was a service provided at markets during the winter when nearly everyone had fleas. From hence comes the name flea-market.

From Vienna, we took a train to Munich, Germany. Here I wanted to see Kaiser Wilhelm's Royal Carriages and the Dachau concentration camp. Both were closed. A fast 150 mph train trip to Mannheim followed. From there, we changed trains and proceeded through Koblenz on to Luxembourg. The next morning, we met the rest of our tour group arriving from New York. Don Kraybill, a former classmate from Eastern Mennonite College days, was in the group. A sociologist, he was a long-time professor at Elizabethtown College who now serves as Provost at Messiah College in Grantham, Pennsylvania. Don has an extensive background both in studying and writing about the Amish. Fannie Erb, assistant editor of the *Sugarcreek Budget*, Sugarcreek, Ohio, was also in the group. Lamar and Lois Ann Mast were the logicians for this annual tour. They are Mennonite historians in their own right. They own a publishing business and bookshop specializing in Amish, Mennonite, and Anabaptist writings. They are from Morgantown, Pennsylvania. Leroy Beachy, from Berlin, Ohio, was our tour guide. He was a key person for those interested in a serious study of Anabaptist history.

The next two days we traveled through Germany to the Alsace area of France. We journeyed through Zweibrücken, Strasbourg, and Obernai to Ste. Marie aux Mines in the Alsace region of France. The three hundredth anniversary of the Amish division was held in Ste. Marie aux Mines. The valley Jacob

Ammann lived in lies just above the city. At the upper end of this large valley was his home. Ammann was one of the key figures in the Swiss Brethren division in 1692. His group's followers became the present-day Amish. The distinct Swiss-like homes that the Swiss Brethren built when they arrived from Switzerland in the early 1670s are still easily recognized. There have been no religious groups with similarities to the Amish in Europe for several generations. Indeed, the European people who still called themselves Amish during the first part of this century would not have been recognized as such by those acquainted with the Amish in America. We visited other communities that were known to have had Amish families. A cemetery we visited near Selm, in the Alsace region of France, had many common names including Schlabach, my mother's maiden name, and Schrock, LaVina's mother's maiden name. One day over lunch, I met a man, Peter Offerlbauer, from Wels, Austria. As a result of that chance meeting, Peter, and his son David, lived in our home for two months the following summer. Following a tour of the wine growing area of Alsace, our tour group moved on to Switzerland. Here we joined Hans Brechbühler, Father's friend. Hans supplemented Leroy Beachy as a local tour guide for the Emmental Valley. With his knowledge of the area and his knowledge of Swiss Brethren history, he was well suited to the task.

We discovered some interesting things while touring. A prayer my parents taught us as toddlers to pray at bedtime is commonly known by the Swiss. Hans learned the same prayer from his parents. We know the Weaver family children were taught this prayer as far back as my great-grandfather. The question begs; was this prayer carried over by our immigrant ancestor in 1764 and passed along for the next eight generations? We had the same question for several German lullabies. Hans told us that "*Schloff Bubbly Schloff*," a lullaby sung to probably the majority of the Amish children in Holmes County, is just as well-known in Switzerland. The word *Mutza* was, I thought, the name for a specific Amish dress coat for men. One night at the end of a yodeling fest, one of the yodelers got up and asked, "*Vo ist my Mutza*." He wore a decorated dress coat. *Lotts Hossa* was another term I thought referred specifically to Amish pants. Guess what! Farmers in several upper Emmental Valley areas still wear them. Hans also sang a ditty in which worldly people wore buttons and the poor and humble wore hooks-and-eyes. It looks to me like most of our traditional Amish ways have their roots in earlier European traditions.

Leroy explained to us that the traditional two weeks of "aus ruffa," before Amish couples get married, stems from an early European custom. Couples wanting to get married had to post a notice at the public building of their town two weeks before the wedding. This was intended to give anyone with an objection to the marriage a chance to lodge it.

From Zurich, I left the group on a train to Munich. I wanted to see the royal carriages and the Dachau concentration camp we had missed earlier. Going through the concentration camp was a sobering experience. The royal carriage exhibit was also worthwhile. A short fast train ride later, I was back in Mannheim. My late arrival necessitated hiring a cab. We had to cross the Rhine River to get to our destination—the Wierhof in the Palatinate. An interesting stay there ensued with a Mennonite family by the name of Galley.

My Present Work

Aꜰᴛᴇʀ ʀᴇᴛᴜʀɴɪɴɢ ꜰʀᴏᴍ Lɪʙᴇʀɪᴀ, ᴍʏ ᴍᴇᴅɪᴄᴀʟ ᴡᴏʀᴋ ᴛᴏᴏᴋ a few unexpected turns. By early 1992, my practice was confined to work as an emergency room physician at Joel Pomerene Hospital in Millersburg, Ohio. Late that winter, Dr. Roy Miller asked me if I would consider helping out temporarily in his practices in Mount Hope and Millersburg. He wanted to be relieved for three months to take additional surgery training in obstetrics and gynecology. Although it was unexpected, I felt honored to be asked. Dr. Miller's staff and patients made the few months there an enjoyable time. Practicing medicine in the community of my birth and among many former friends and acquaintances was a new and gratifying experience. In mid-June, before I finished in Dr. Miller's office, the Millersburg community was shocked by the unexpected death of Dr. Robert Huston. Dr. Huston had practiced in Millersburg for 32 years. He had a large family practice and was serving as medical direc-

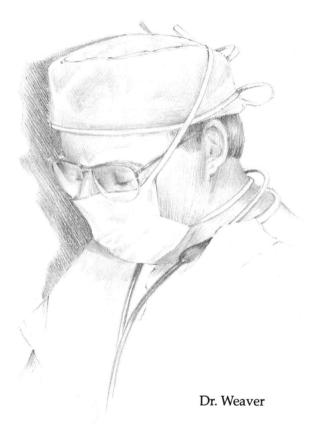

Dr. Weaver

tor of the hospital at the time of his death. Because of under-staffing in the surgery department, he was also doing surgery.

Following his death, I was asked to consider providing coverage for the Huston practice until a doctor was recruited to permanently replace him. After a lot of indecision, I agreed to help out for six to twelve months. These plans were extended to two years when a replacement couldn't be found the first year. During the two years in Dr. Huston's office, I continued to work one or two shifts a week in the emergency room. Mrs. Huston and the secretarial and nursing staff made the two-year period a pleasant and rewarding time. While there, I experienced reunions with many friends and family members who were former acquaintances. These folks, and the friendships formed with new patients, made leaving the practice a little perplexing. I left the practice and staff with a tinge of guilt and sadness. Dr. Steve Clutter, formerly from Danville, came to take over the practice in July 1994. He had just completed his residency training in Internal Medicine in Toledo.

Plans for LaVina's and my wedding, buying and readying a house, and starting in the Huston practice, kept me busy the summer and fall of 1992. Later in November, we were married. During the following winter and spring, Father's health deteriorated until he passed away in May. Since leaving the Huston practice, I have worked full-time in the emergency room again.

Like my other medical practice experiences, I have found emergency room work challenging and satisfying. Medical practice here in Holmes County has broadened my field of experiences. In practicing medicine in Virginia for twenty years, I never once cared for a patient with hemophilia. Since coming back to Ohio, I have cared for several hundred hemophilia patients. It is a genetically transmitted disorder found among the Amish of Holmes County. Work as an emergency room doc-

tor is often interesting and challenging. One never knows what the day's work will involve. Usually a variety of events can be expected. A majority of the patients are non-emergency cases and are seen because we are their only access to treatment, or are more convenient. On a busy day, when we have a wide variety of problems, I occasionally keep problem lists for the shift.

Following is an actual list of patient problems encountered over two separate twelve-hour shifts:

2 ear infections
3 children with high fevers
1 case of poison ivy
1 child who had eaten an unknown wild mushroom
1 bladder infection
3 sore throats
2 people with bronchitis
1 stroke
1 pneumonia
1 acute asthma attack
1 acute gall bladder attack
2 kidney stone patients
2 congestive heart failure patients
2 heart attack patients
1 hand caught in a machine at work
1 broken arm
2 patients with broken ribs
2 patients with sprained ankles
5 patients with lacerations
4 patients involved in two motor vehicle accidents

In spite of their sober appearance, many of my Amish friends and relatives have a keen sense of humor. I was recently reminded of this when a middle aged Amish lady came into the emergency room to have a facial laceration sutured. Her husband arrived after we were repairing the injury, and promptly fainted. While he was being assisted on the floor, his wife remarked, "Don't worry, he doesn't function much better than that on his good days."

Our emergency room is not like the program dramatized on television, but our staff has its share of challenging, exciting, and heart-breaking days. We see patients from one-day-old to one hundred years old and all the years in between. Trying to stay up-to-date with medicine's frontiers is an exciting challenge. It is a job never done. The combined years of experience found in a skilled nursing staff and good medical staff consultants make the work gratifying although not always easy. Most of our major acute trauma, and all of our cardiovascular surgery and neurosurgery patients, are transferred to larger medical centers. Both ground and helicopter transport are used depending on the individual case. Our community is fortunate to have a well-trained and organized rescue squad.

Our Emergency Room charge nurse, Carol Maurer, frequently shares musings of wit and wisdom on our bulletin board. I was reminded of one of them recently. "Wisdom doesn't necessarily come with age, some people grow old without it." I have had a wide variety of experiences in my life, but regarding being wise, may the above serve as my disclaimer. I guess I am like the old dirt shovel I saw an auctioneer try to sell recently. In the end, he got five dollars for it, but only after claiming that its value was much increased by its great experience.

Several things on the back burner are awaiting my attention. The first one is restoration of the Conestoga wagon in which one of my paternal great-grandmothers is alleged to have come to Ohio. Pencil sketching, painting, and wood carving classes—something I have long wanted to do—are hopefully around the corner. High on the wish-list of travel destinations for the future are South Africa and Cuba. Hopefully, voluntary medical assignments will continue to be a part of our future endeavors. We anticipate continued contact with Liberia, where we are presently involved in several projects.

The Bridge at Sinkor

BECAUSE I DELIBERATELY AVOIDED MAKING MY STORY A statement of faith, I feel a need to comment on that aspect of my life at this time. In doing this, I want to share with my readers an encounter I had with a man in Liberia in 1991.

I saw myself in a somewhat different light before I met the man from the bridge at Sinkor. The setting was early March 1991, several weeks after I arrived in Monrovia, Liberia, in western Africa. I met this man, his wife, and five of their seven children at one of our clinics. He introduced his family by saying, "We are here only by the grace of God." I paused to silently acknowledge what he had said before falling into my how-can-I-help-you-today mode. The waiting rooms were full and the halls lined with people waiting to be seen. He ignored my opening by saying, "You don't understand. God, by a miracle, saved my wife, my seven children, and my life."

He then went on to tell me how one night, several months earlier, he and his family crept through the military lines into the city. They were trying to flee from the rampant killings going on in the countryside. Coming into the city from the southeast they avoided confrontation by taking side roads and avoiding areas where they heard shooting. As they neared the downtown area, they were joined by other refugees. About the same time, armed men started to appear along the streets. Soon they found themselves being funneled onto the road leading to Bushrod Island.

To get to the island, one first had to cross the bridge at Sinkor. It was a long bridge. As the family neared the bridge, they heard shooting at the far end. There, another faction of rebels were screening all the refugees crossing the bridge. As they neared the far end of the bridge, they saw some of the people being taken aside and shot. When armed men kept the people from turning back, the family started praying silently as their turn neared.

When the time for their interview arrived, the man was led to an officer sitting on a chair at the side of the bridge. Before he quite reached the officer, he started to open his mouth to speak. Before he could say anything, the officer angrily shouted at him to shut his mouth. The officer then had one of the soldiers bring the man's wife to him. After a period of angry questioning, the officer motioned the family to cross to Bushrod Island.

After they distanced themselves from the bridge, the family stopped to get their bearings. There they were told that the rebels at the bridge were killing anyone they suspected of coming from the Krahn Tribe. They identified the Krahn people by their distinct dialect. The officer apparently suspected that the man was trying to cover for his wife when he seemed to want to talk too soon. As it turned out, the man was from the Krahn Tribe and his wife was from another tribe. Had the man been allowed to talk, the whole family would have been killed. Thus it was that the man from the bridge at Sinkor wanted me to acknowledge the God that saved him and his family.

So in closing, I want—with the man from the bridge at Sinkor—to acknowledge my faith. I claim God as creator of the universe and all that is in it. I claim Jesus Christ, the son of God, as my Lord. I believe the Holy Spirit is the medium God uses to relate to his people. I believe in doing to others what I would have others do to me. Where my example has fallen short, I accept responsibility and ask those offended, and God, to forgive me. "We were taught well by word and example," is the legacy I hope to leave to my children and grandchildren.

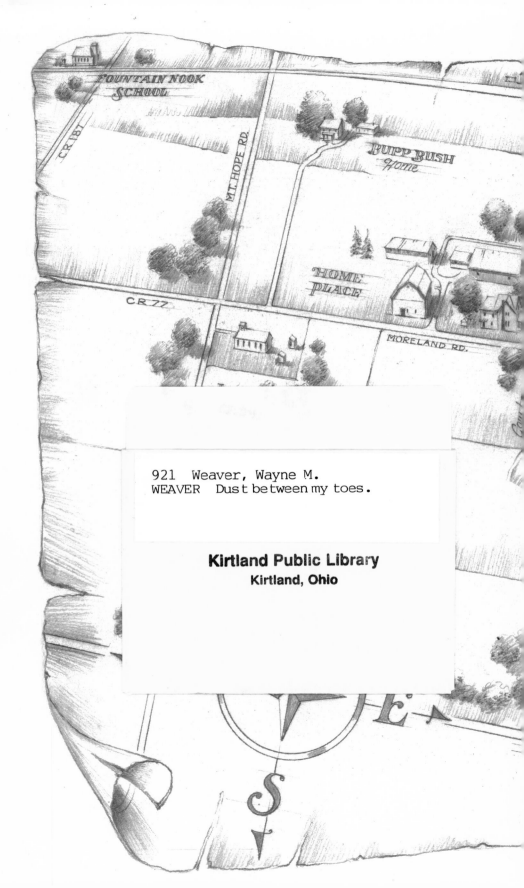